Other titles by Dorothy M. Johnson
available in Bison Books editions

ALL THE BUFFALO RETURNING

BUFFALO WOMAN

THE HANGING TREE

INDIAN COUNTRY

SOME
WENT
WEST

Dorothy M. Johnson

ILLUSTRATED WITH PHOTOGRAPHS

Introduction to the Bison Books edition
by Virginia Scharff

UNIVERSITY OF NEBRASKA PRESS
LINCOLN

© 1965 by Dorothy M. Johnson
Introduction © 1997 by the University of Nebraska Press
All rights reserved
Manufactured in the United States of America

♾ The paper in this book meets the minimum requirements of American National Standard for Information Sciences—Permanence of Paper for Printed Library Materials, ANSI Z39.48-1984.

First Bison Books printing: 1997

Library of Congress Cataloging-in-Publication Data
Johnson, Dorothy M.
Some went west / Dorothy M. Johnson; introduction to the Bison Books edition by Virginia Scharff.
p.   cm.
Originally published: New York: Dodd, Mead & Co., 1965.
Includes bibliographical references and index.
Summary: Describes the lives and varied experiences of some of the many women who traveled across the American West, including Cynthia Ann Parker, Mary Richardson Walker, Harriet Sanders, Maria Virginia Slade, and Elizabeth Custer.
ISBN 0-8032-7598-6 (pbk: alk. paper)
1. Women pioneers—West (U.S.)—History—Juvenile literature.
2. West (U.S.)—History—Juvenile literature.   [1. Frontier and pioneer life—West (U.S.)   2. Women—Biography.   3. West (U.S.)—History.]
I. Title.
F596.J48   1997
978—dc21
97-1509   CIP
AC

Reprinted from the original 1965 edition by Dodd, Mead & Company, New York.

This book is dedicated to

my Aunt Mattie,

Mrs. Homer Taggart, Midland, South Dakota

Introduction

Virginia Scharff

What if we were to put in a single room all the women whose stories you are about to read? What, I wonder, would they have to say to one another? They are an amazingly diverse lot— missionaries and tourists, wives of outlaws and a general's widow, ranchers and reformers, doctors and nuns. Some you will meet as children and accompany on short, but harrowing journeys. Others you will follow through long, sometimes tortuous lives. In some of these women, boldness looks like bravery, but in others, it seems mere ignorance or recklessness. What in the world do they have in common?

They all moved. And they all made their journeys into and through the place we call the American West.

The West is a country of trails deeply etched by women's footsteps. Look at where they walked, and rode, and lived. Look at the work they did, at the stakes they claimed and the worlds they built. They were not always wise, or admirable. They were as often blind or foolish or fearful as brave and resourceful. Some of them persisted in loving men who were beastly to them. But read the stories in this book and you will discover, in an almost visceral way, how women's hard work made this place called the American West what it has been, and what it is. We did not always know where those women were, or where they went, or how to find them; writers like Dorothy M. Johnson had to show the way.

Johnson was a western girl herself, born in McGregor, Iowa, in 1905. But she learned early the ways of the road, moving to Whitefish, Montana, where she graduated from high school. Bright and ambitious, she was soon off to Missoula to go to college at what is now the University of Montana. Even then, it seems, she knew she could write, contributing pieces to *The Frontier*, the campus literary magazine.

Johnson graduated from Montana in 1928, but she was not fully equipped to begin life as a writer. As Virginia Woolf was just then explaining to women students at English colleges, women who will write must have money and a room of their own. Dorothy Johnson had to make a living. She set off in search of work as a stenographer, landing first in Okanogan, Washington, and later in Menasha, Wisconsin. Did years of taking down other people's words try Johnson's patience? Did this woman who loved to write feel tempted, all the time, to change this or that, to make it sound better?

By 1935, she would have her chance to tinker with words, moving to New York to work for the Gregg and Farrell Publishing Companies as a magazine editor. Over the next fifteen years, she honed her own skills while she polished other people's writing, and began to publish short stories and magazine articles. She also began to study, from the vantage point of New York, the history and culture of Plains Indians.

You might say Dorothy Johnson went east, but it didn't take. She returned to Whitefish, to edit her hometown newspaper and to put together a collection of short stories titled *Indian Country*, published simultaneously in hard cover and paperback in 1953. In that oft-reprinted volume, Johnson established herself as an unsentimental and respectful chronicler of Indian life. The most famous of those stories, "A Man Called Horse," was made into a landmark western movie in 1970, eight years after another of her celebrated stories, "The Man Who Shot Liberty Valance," made a blockbuster transition to the screen.

In 1953, she moved again, to Missoula, to teach journalism at the University of Montana. She continued to produce both western short stories and nonfiction, but turned her attention to writing books aimed at young readers. She did not, however, entirely abandon adult audiences, and her last works of fiction, *Buffalo Woman* (1977) and *All the Buffalo Returning* (1979) offered realistic, sympathetic portraits of everyday life among the Oglala band of the Lakotas. Over the course of a long and prolific career, she won virtually every award available to western writers, including the coveted Western Heritage Wrangler Award from the National Cowboy Hall of Fame.

When Johnson published *Some Went West* in 1965, you'd have had to look long and hard for something to read about women in the American West. In 1958, historian and novelist Dee Brown published *The Gentle Tamers*, depicting white women as civilizing bearers of culture to a raw, wild country. A small number of less ambitious books pictured pioneer women as work-worn drudges. But Dorothy Johnson knew that nobody is only one thing. People's motives and actions are complicated; people change. Women are no different from men in these regards, but their lives often take different courses from men's lives. Gender shapes people's experience of marriage and family, rights and property, war and peace, land and movement. In American history, women's relations to all those things have been restrictive, in ways men's have not. Telling their stories helps to reveal some of the complicated ways in which men's and women's experiences and opportunities have diverged.

Consider the first person you will meet in these pages, Cynthia Ann Parker. She was a white woman, captured and adopted by Comanches. She would marry a Comanche man and bear a son, Quanah, who became a leader of his people. She learned to love, and to think herself one of those people. But she was torn from them in a second captivity by whites who mistakenly believed they were rescuing her. Her son Quanah crossed into the white world with a willingness his mother did not share, perhaps in part because the former warrior had opportunities, as a man, to establish for himself a new way of life as a landholding rancher. To see her story clearly, Dorothy Johnson had to look beyond the simple formulas of western tales of cowboys and Indian warriors.

Dorothy Johnson understood that women's stories were complex, their decisions and motives sometimes inexplicable. How else can we comprehend Mary Walker's lifelong devotion to the abusive Elkana, or the almost unthinkable courage and resourcefulness of Bethenia Owens Adair? Johnson also shows us the ironies in these stories. The German sisters, she explains, would never have suffered so much as captives of a band of Cheyennes had the U.S.

Army not been chasing them. Johnson also reminds us that Elizabeth Custer, the person almost singlehandedly responsible for George Armstrong Custer's heroic reputation, was "always aware ... that if one little thing went wrong, somebody—perhaps her own husband—would kill her."

These are thinking women, and they are working women. Perhaps Johnson's greatest contribution, in this volume, was to see the ways women's work shaped their world. Even fun-loving Harriet Sanders worked her way across the continent, pinning her wet laundry to the wagon top to let it dry as the train moved, learning the hard way that leaving tin pans in the hot sun would result in burnt fingers before the baking even began. Young Catherine German learned from her Cheyenne captors how to sew with buffalo sinew and a bone needle. Bethenia Owens' mother carried flax seed all the way to Oregon, chopped the sod with an ax, hoed her cherished crop to maturity. She got a neighbor to make her a spinning wheel, spun the thread so that the family could sew shoes, traded her flax with Indians who knew what fine fishing nets that thread would make. For Grace McCance, as for countless others, carrying water was a perpetual burden, and doing the weekly washing was a hot, heavy, backbreaking job. Johnson makes us feel very clearly the joy of the woman whose husband dug a well near the house, the almost unthinkable privilege of the wife who even had a pump in her kitchen! Johnson was fascinated with what she called "details of domestic arrangements," and she described brilliantly the women's work that went into the necessities of life—soap, starch, thread, bread.

As we near the end of the twentieth century, the idea that western stories are full of irony and complexity, and even full of flesh-and-blood, hardworking women, is nothing new to us. But in the 1960s, when the television programs "Gunsmoke" and "Bonanza" thrilled millions, both subtlety and women were largely missing from western narratives. Readers today have developed a keen awareness of racial stereotypes and insensitive language, and we should not be surprised to find some of both in this book. Neither should we be surprised to find that we can learn far more about some of the women Johnson sketches here (Isabella Bird, Nannie Alderson, and others) by reading elsewhere their own stories, in their own words.

But every journey has to begin somewhere. In 1965, Americans were only very dimly aware that among those who "went west" were women whose history mattered. Dorothy Johnson had, and has, something important to say. None of the women you will encounter in these pages dreamed, when she started out, where she might end. This book is a good place to start an intellectual journey whose destination we certainly cannot predict, perhaps cannot yet imagine.

Acknowledgments

My sincere thanks for the special help given by these nice people:

Fay Alderson, Sheridan, Wyoming; Mattie Taggart, Midland, South Dakota; Sister Rita of the Sacred Heart, President of the College of Great Falls, Montana; Emma Briscoe, Chairman, Home Economics Department, Montana State University; William Bertsche, Great Falls; Virginia W. Johnson, Missoula, Montana; Alberta Pantle, Librarian, Kansas State Historical Society; Enid T. Thompson, Librarian, The State Historical Society of Colorado; Mary K. Dempsey, Librarian, Montana Historical Society; Helen Edwards, White Tail Ranch, Ovando, Montana; Henry Parker Woods, Missoula, Montana.

Preface

Until the whole continental United States was really settled and there were no frontiers any more, people kept moving westward. What kind of people were they?

It has been said that the cowards never started, and the weaklings fell by the way. The editor of Montana's first newspaper looked around him thoughtfully a century ago and wrote, "No average people live in these regions."

We can be sure of this about the men and women who settled and lived and died beyond the limits of peaceful civilization: They weren't cowards, they weren't weaklings, and they weren't average.

Thousands of young men without family responsibilities went west seeking adventure and hoping for riches. They all found adventure, a few became prosperous, and many were never heard from again. They died of wounds or sickness.

During the various gold rushes, thousands of family men, too, left home and rode west, intending to return—and many of them were never heard from again, either.

Those were the adventurers. The settlers were a different breed. They hoped to find a better living than they had left behind. They went west to stay. They took their wives and children along; they took civilization with them. They built stable communities.

Most pioneer women went west because their husbands needed them. There must have been countless scenes like this: A man and a woman facing each other across the kitchen table late at night, after the children were in bed. The man had broken the news that he wanted to go west and start all over again. "Things will be better for us there," he kept saying. "I've talked to men who know."

"But—leave everything?" his wife asked fearfully. "Leave all our folks? Never see them again?" She had dozens of arguments for not going.

Then, crying because she couldn't help herself, she said at last, "Well, all right, if that's what you think we should do."

After all the plans were made and the family belongings packed (and beloved treasures given away because there wasn't room in the wagon to take them), there were the last farewells, the partings from friends and relatives who would probably never be seen again. There were the women left behind, holding aprons to their eyes to wipe away tears and to hide the sight of the great covered wagon pulling out toward unknown perils. There were the familiar voices crying, "Now be sure to write!"

Be sure to write—the heartbreaking, unnecessary reminder, the thing to say in parting when there's nothing else left to say.

Leaving the familiar, beloved places and people was harder for women than for men. Women are conservative, less likely to seek adventure for its own sake. Most women who went west had just one reason: Their men wanted to go.

These women had a stabilizing influence in the communities they helped build. They objected to the wild ways of the frontier West; no doubt they complained and even nagged—until the wildness was tamed and their children were safe.

This book is about some of the women who went west. They may not have felt heroic, but they weren't cowards. They were not all physically strong, but they weren't weaklings in spirit. And they certainly weren't average, except in this: They loyally went along because they were needed. Women still do this. Sometimes courage is only normal.

Dorothy M. Johnson

Contents

I

Some Were Captured by Indians

Cynthia Ann Parker, Fanny Kelly, and the German Sisters

NONE OF THE PIONEERS who kept moving the American frontier westward expected anything terrible to happen to them personally. They knew there was danger, of course, and prepared for it as well as they could. Hardship was familiar to most of them, even back home. But disaster is something that is supposed to strike somebody else.

For Cynthia Ann Parker, disaster struck twice—first when she was nine years old and again when she was thirty-three.

When John Parker and his large family emigrated from Illinois to Texas in 1833, none of them foresaw horror. They settled down to farm about forty-five miles west of Fort Houston. Prudently they built a high log stockade around their cluster of cabins, as protection against possible Indian attacks.

Grandfather John Parker and his wife had three sons, James, Silas, and Benjamin. James had two married daughters, Rachel Plummer and Sarah Nixon. All of them had families, each living in its own small, dirt-floored cabin. About thirty-four persons, including the Parkers, lived inside the stockade. They called the place Fort Parker. Several of these people were destined for tragedy.

Whenever danger from Indians threatened, the men hurried to drive their livestock into the protecting fort, seized their weapons, and prepared to defend their families.

But on May 19, 1836, danger moved too fast. Several of the men were working in the fields when a big war party of Comanche and Kiowa Indians rode to the attack.

Terrible confusion followed. Many of the whites were killed and scalped.

When the Indians rode away, yelling in triumph, the survivors of Fort Parker were hiding in the brush. After great hardships, they reached a settlement some fifty miles away.

But with the Indians rode five terrified captives: Mrs. Rachel Plummer and her baby son, James, eighteen months old; Mrs. Elizabeth Kellogg; Cynthia Ann Parker, aged nine; and her six-year-old brother, John.

Mrs. Kellogg was ransomed six months later for one hundred and fifty dollars and was returned to her family.

Rachel Plummer suffered through some ghastly experiences. Her baby was taken from her, and she never knew what became of him. He was rescued several years later, but she was dead by that time. At the time of her capture, she was three months pregnant. After that baby was born, the Indians brutally killed it.

Rachel's father, James Parker, made five long journeys in three years, searching for her. Grim and determined, he went without food for days at a time, always in danger. When his horse dropped and his boots wore out, his feet left blood stains as he walked.

On February 18, 1838, he reclaimed his lost daughter. Rachel had been rescued by some traders from Santa Fe and had been taken to Independence, Missouri. Her health was ruined by the privations she had undergone, and she did not live very long—but she died among her own people.

In January, 1843, James Parker heard that two white boys had been brought to Fort Gibson. He hurried to meet them, hoping that they were the missing James, Rachel's son, and John, Cynthia Ann's brother, captured seven years before.

The boys were as frightened as wild animals, and like wild animals they tried to run away from the old man who wanted to stare into their faces. They were not expecting kind treatment from him or anyone else.

He asked them questions, but they remembered almost no English. But grim old James Parker recognized the younger one because he looked like his dead mother, Rachel, and he knew that the older boy must be Cynthia Ann's brother. James took them both home.

Still missing was Cynthia Ann, now sixteen years old. Where was she? No white man knew, but all of them watched for her when they saw Indians, and they listened to stories that might bring news.

Three years after the two boys were reclaimed, an army officer visiting a Comanche Indian camp saw a young woman who was not an Indian, although she lived with them and dressed like them. The officer was sure that she was the missing Parker girl. He offered rich ransom for her: a dozen mules and several hundred dollars' worth of trade goods. But Cynthia Ann, nineteen now, was afraid of him. She ran away and hid, as any other girl in the tribe would have done.

A year later she was seen again. She had married and did not want to be rescued.

She was twenty-four the next time some traders recognized her. She had babies and looked like a Comanche—except that her eyes were blue. She spoke no English. The men asked, through an interpreter, whether she wanted to go back to her people. They said later that her lips quivered, but aside from this she did not reply.

In December, 1860, a force of Texas Rangers attacked a camp of Comanches, and the Battle of Pease River ensued. The Rangers rode and shouted, the Indians scurried, and there was much shooting on both sides. Ranger Captain Sul Ross fired at an Indian warrior on horseback, who had a young Indian girl on the horse behind him, clinging to him as he tried to escape. The shot struck the girl, who toppled off the horse, carrying the warrior with her. He leaped to his feet and fired back.

A bullet from Captain Ross's gun broke the warrior's right arm, and two more bullets entered his body, wounding him mortally.

The Indian walked with dignity to a tree, leaned against it, and began to sing his death song. A soldier killed him with a blast from a shotgun. The dead man was Peta Nocona, a Comanche war chief, the husband of Cynthia Ann Parker.

Meanwhile, another soldier had captured her. Riding a horse, with her baby daughter in her arms, she surrendered to keep from being killed. Her captor took a long look. She was filthy dirty, and her skin was brown and her hair was dark (as a child, she had been blonde), but her eyes were blue.

Thus, for the second time, Cynthia Ann was wrenched from people she loved. All that night after her capture by the Rangers she cried for her dead husband and her two missing sons; she asked whether they were dead, too, but nobody knew. Captain Ross returned her to the white settlements, where she was reunited with members of the Parker family— but she cried continuously. Her relatives talked to her, asking questions about her capture. She would not answer; she did not understand English. But she did recognize her childhood name, Cynthia. Her Indian name was Preloch, and she had been a Comanche for twenty-four years.

Only one photograph was ever made of Preloch, who had been Cynthia Ann. She is nursing her infant daughter, and she is not smiling. She never smiled again after she was taken from the Comanches.

Her relatives did the best they could for her. One of them became her guardian. The state of Texas granted her some land and a pension of one hundred dollars a year.

Once captured, once rescued—that was the way the Parkers and the other whites thought about Cynthia Ann. But she herself must have felt that she had been captured twice by enemies and never rescued at all. And the second captivity must have been the worse, for this time she lost her two sons and the war chief who was her husband. She was not a white woman any more except by blood. She was an Indian woman; she had learned in childhood to accept Indian customs.

Constantly she grieved for her lost sons. She even undertook to learn English when the Parkers promised that if she would do that she could visit her Indian people and try to find her two boys. But by this time Texas was engaged in the Civil War, and she could not travel. She learned to spin and weave to help with the war effort, always dreaming of searching for her sons.

Her little girl died while the war was still going on. Cynthia grieved anew and was sent to live with a sister in another county. In 1864, before the war ended, she died of grippe— or perhaps from a broken heart. She was thirty-seven years old.

And what of her sons? One of them, called Pecos, died. The other, Quanah, became very famous. She would have been proud of him if she had lived to know of it. Quanah was about fourteen when his father was killed and his mother was captured by the Texas Rangers.

Quanah was both courageous and wise. He became a subchief of a Comanche band that was very hostile to the whites. He fought valiantly in many battles. As long as it seemed possible to the Indians that they might yet drive the white men off their buffalo range and go on living as they had always lived, Quanah fought.

In 1867, he refused to sign a treaty that would have put his people on a limited reservation to be ruled by the white man's government. His Kwahadi Comanches still rode free —but the white men kept moving in and killing the buffalo on which the Indians depended.

Immense herds of buffalo—so many that nobody could tell how many millions there were—had grazed on the rich grass of the prairies for centuries. They were the wild cattle of the Indians, but difficult to kill when all the hunters went on foot. When horses were brought to the North American continent by the Spanish explorers in the sixteenth century, some of them got away, and the Indians learned how to capture them and ride them. This entirely changed the Indians' way of life. Now they could pursue the buffalo, and they came to depend on these great, shaggy animals for almost everything. The hides became warm bedding and covers for their houses—those ingenious, collapsible, comfortable shelters called tepees. (A wigwam is not the same thing at all. Wigwams were made of bark and were used by forest-dwelling tribes farther east.) Bones became tools and implements. Various of the inner parts were used for containers. The sinews took the place of thread. The woolly fur had its uses. And the meat—the meat was the staff of life, whether fresh or dried to make nutritious pemmican.

The westward-moving white people threatened this seemingly endless supply of everything that the Indians of the Plains needed for comfort and food. Is it any wonder that they learned to resent the white men's encroachment on their vast hunting grounds? When hunting was poor, they starved.

In 1874, Quanah knew that his people must make a great decision. All the Indians of the southern plains would have to join together in driving out the whites, or else they must give up.

Most dangerous to the Indians' welfare were the hide hunters, men who made a business of slaughtering buffalo by the thousands and selling their hides to be shipped to the eastern United States to be made into leather.

At a great gathering of Indians, it was agreed that the hide hunters must be killed. Quanah led the Comanches, while chiefs named Lone Wolf and Stone Calf led the Kiowas and the Cheyennes. The first place they hoped to wipe out was a buffalo hunters' camp at Adobe Walls. Seven hundred Indians attacked before dawn on June 27, 1874.

Quanah kept the attack going for three days, while the beleagured white men fought back. After Quanah's best warriors had been killed and he had been wounded in the shoulder, he gave up and led his fighting men away.

Cynthia Ann's warrior son saw that there was no use fighting any more. There were too many white men in Indian country now. When his people were finally forced to surrender, Quanah did his best to get favorable promises from the victorious whites. He led his people to the reservation that the United States Government said they must occupy, but he was always bitter toward President William McKinley for allotting only 160 acres of land to each Indian—it wasn't enough to enable anyone to earn a living.

It is terribly hard for any people to be forced to change their ancient customs suddenly. It was as hard for the Indians of the plains to give up their way of life, which depended on hunting buffalo and moving their tepee villages often, as it would be for a rural community of white people to leave their farms and have to depend on hunting for a living.

But Quanah, a wise leader of his defeated people, said, "If my mother could learn the ways of the Indians, I can learn the ways of the white man." He visited Cynthia Ann's relatives and took their name. He was known thereafter as Quanah Parker.

He learned white man's ways and became a prosperous rancher. He made at least three trips to Washington, D. C., to argue for the rights of his people, and he rode in President Theodore Roosevelt's inaugural parade in 1905.

After the Comanches accepted the idea of living on a reservation, Quanah deeply desired that his mother's body be buried there. In 1910, Congress authorized the removal of her body and that of her little girl to a cemetery at Cache, Oklahoma.

Quanah died a year later and was buried beside his mother.

There is a monument to Cynthia Ann, who had become Preloch, on the old reservation, and one to her great son, Quanah. There is another marker on the site of her capture by Sul Ross near Crowell, Texas. A town in the Texas Panhandle is named Quanah. And Parker County, in north central Texas, is named for the family that entered our history through disaster and tragedy.

*   *   *

Many of the white women who were captured by Indians were never heard from again, but some who yearned for rescue were fortunate and were returned to their own people. Fanny Kelly was one of these.

Fanny was only nineteen when she was captured by a band of Ogallala Sioux Indians. Her experiences made her wise beyond her years. During her captivity, she suffered and despaired, living in constant terror—but she did not want to die.

After she was rescued, many people told her they thought death would have been preferable to life with such bleak prospects as she had as a captive, but Fanny knew better. In the book she wrote later, *Narrative of My Captivity Among the Sioux Indians,* she commented, "It is only those who have looked over the dark abyss of death who know how the soul shrinks from meeting the unknown future. Experience is a grand teacher, and we were then in her school and learned that while hope offers the faintest token of refuge, we pause upon the fearful brink of eternity and look back for rescue."

Her maiden name was Wiggins, and she was born in Canada in 1845. The family moved to Geneva, Kansas, in 1856, and in November, 1863, she married Josiah Kelly, a young veteran of the Civil War. His health was not good; he hoped to regain it in the far West, and so on May 17, 1864, they set out in a covered wagon for Idaho Territory. With them went a five-year-old girl, Mary, the child of Fanny's older sister. Altogether, there were five wagons in their train, and the group consisted of eleven people, including a couple named Larimer, who had a boy eight years old.

We have been told often about the hardships of the covered-wagon pioneers, and they did endure hardships—but like many other women, Fanny remembered the journey as a delightful, extended camping trip. There were long, work-free hours for Fanny and Mrs. Larimer to gather flowers with the children, to pick berries, to savor new experiences, or just to admire the beauties of the prairie. For amusement, the emigrants sang or read, wrote letters home, or simply talked. Days were hot, but in the evening the air cooled and was laden with the odor of prairie flowers, which carpeted the earth with color.

On Sundays they rested and had a church service, with a sermon preached by a minister in the party.

At Fort Laramie they were assured that there was no danger from Indians. Serenely they continued on their way —but on the twelfth day of July, about eighty miles farther on, horror engulfed them. Suddenly the cliffs above them were covered with a party of some 250 Sioux Indians, whooping and painted for war. The Indians fired a volley of shots as a signal for the wagon train to stop.

The white men corralled the wagons, and Josiah Kelly, leader of the train, prepared for defense. Fanny pleaded with him not to fire. One shot, she was sure, would start an unequal battle that would end in massacre. She was frantic with fear for little Mary, who had an ungovernable dread of Indians. Fanny had tried to convince her that there was no danger. But here it was.

The whites gave the Indians everything they demanded— Mr. Kelly's favorite saddle horse, trade goods (with which they had expected to make a profit in the mining camps of Idaho), clothing, food. The Indians grew more insolent, and the emigrants tried to pacify them. Then the danger seemed to be over. The chief motioned to indicate that the wagons should move on.

As the wagons approached a rocky glen, from which escape would be impossible, Josiah Kelly called a halt. The Indians told him they wanted a feast; after that, they would go away. Two Negro menservants who had worked for the Kellys for a long time were terrified, because they had once been slaves in another Indian tribe, but they set to work preparing supper. The other men in the party built a fire, unloaded provisions from the wagon, and looked after the horses.

Suddenly the Sioux fired their guns and started yelling.

Fanny Kelly saw three of the men in her party die almost at her feet, shot with rifle balls or pierced with arrows. In the confusion and gun smoke, she could not see where her husband was.

The yelling Indians tore open the things in the covered wagons, destroyed or scattered them, and set them afire. Two fierce warriors seized Fanny by the hands and threw her to the ground so hard that she suffered for a long time afterward. When she could get up, she took little Mary in her arms and begged the chief to protect Mrs. Larimer, the two children, and herself.

A young Indian named Wechela did something kind for Fanny: he brought her some things that had been scattered from her wagon, including a bunch of letters. She hid these in her clothing, because she suddenly had an idea that they might be useful.

The four captives—Fanny, clutching Mary before her on a crippled horse, and Mrs. Larimer with her little boy on another horse—started out to an unknown destination with the triumphant Sioux driving them.

When it was dark, Fanny Kelly whispered earnestly to her niece: "We're only a few miles from where we camped. You can wade the stream we crossed. I've been dropping pieces of my letters as we rode. You follow them back, and then you can get away. When you get to the wagon trail, someone will find you and take care of you."

Fanny hoped that was true. Many emigrant wagons did follow that road. Some members of her party had escaped to carry word of the attack to the nearest fort. She hoped that searchers would come out. Her heart was torn at the idea of sending the little girl back to wander alone, following the scattered pieces of paper, but the situation was desperate. This was the best solution she could think of.

"Now I'm going to let you down off the horse," she told
the child, "and you must lie on the ground and hide until
you're sure the Indians have all gone on. If I can, I'll follow
you."

She kissed little Mary and gently dropped her to the
ground.

A little later, in the darkness, Fanny carefully slipped off
the horse and hid. But one of the Indians noticed her ab-
sence and shouted to the others. Forty or fifty of the warriors
rode over the ground, and the horses, sensing Fanny's presence, reared in fear and gave her away.

Fanny told her angry captors that Mary had fallen asleep
and had dropped off the horse and that she was only trying
to find the child. Now she could not go back to catch up with
Mary, and she did not know whether Josiah was alive or
dead.

One night Mrs. Larimer and her boy were taken away, and
after that Fanny was more desperately afraid than ever. She
was all alone among her captors. The Sioux constantly threatened to kill her. She pacified them by giving them all the
money she had hidden away in her clothing—one hundred
and twenty dollars. They understood what money was and
seemed pleased with the gift.

At first she slept on the ground with no bed at all, and
nobody gave her any food, but she was too sick with fear to
want to eat. The first food she got was a chunk of raw antelope meat.

When the war party reached the place where the tepee
village was located, the men stopped to dress up for a triumphal entry. Many of them put on garments taken from the
emigrant wagons—Fanny saw one fierce fellow wearing her
own hat, and another carried a dainty parasol. Ottawa, the
chief, whose property she had become, looked ferocious in a

feathered headdress, with his face painted red and black and his eyes circled with yellow. He wore a shirt of buckskin trimmed with scalp locks, and he wrapped himself in a bright, pieced quilt from one of the wagons.

The chief's six wives were naturally astonished when he brought Fanny into their tepee. They were more interested, however, in the distribution of the things he had brought from the wagons. They got into a fight about which one should have what; the senior wife grabbed her knife and yelled threats at the others; and the chief gave them a harsh scolding that quieted all of them.

Fanny was terrified of the women, but they were curious about her, examined her clothing, and spoke kindly in signs. When they saw how bruised she was, from a fall from her crippled horse, they dressed her wounds as well as they could. The chief even gave her his little daughter, Yellow Bird, to take the place of her lost Mary.

The chief took Fanny to several feasts, wanting to show off his captive, and at last she had a comfortable bed of furs.

Thirteen days after the attack on the wagons, the Indians held a big celebration because none of their men had been killed. Fanny had a seat of honor and listened to many speeches, trembling with fear because she suspected that they intended some horrible fate for her.

The feast that followed featured dog stew. There was plenty of meat in the camp, but Fanny understood that the Indians ate dog because of some religious custom. She choked down enough of it to satisfy them that she was being polite. The women let her know that she was highly honored in being permitted to eat with the men, but it was an honor she would happily have gone without.

In the victory dance that followed, she had to stand and

hold a pole from which human scalps dangled while the men leaped and stamped around her.

Soon the whole village moved to another place. Scared as she was, Fanny took an interest in what she saw. The Sioux, like other tribes on the Plains, lived by hunting, and all their property had to be portable so they could follow the buffalo herds. They had no permanent villages at all.

This time the warriors were going to fight white soldiers, so the women, children, and old people were being sent to a place of safety. The women took down the tepee poles and wrapped up the tepee covers, which were made of hides sewed together with sinew. Both horses and dogs pulled travois loaded with bundles and sometimes with a child or two.

A travois, or "pony drag," is made by tying one end of a pole to each side of a horse so that the loose ends drag on the ground behind the animal. This makes a sloping platform on which bundles can be fastened. Fanny saw big dogs used for freight animals, too, each with a heavy iron kettle hanging on one side and a baby in its carrier on the other, for balance.

Later Fanny learned that the warriors' purpose was to attack General Alfred Sully's army, which was pursuing the Indians. They returned three days later and held a victory ceremony by torchlight, with furious dancing and yelling. Again Fanny had to participate, shuddering at the fresh scalps dangling from the pole she held.

In her book she gave a clear and sensible explanation of the Indians' bitter antipathy toward any invasion of their country by white men: "The felling of timber, or killing of buffalo, or traveling of a [wagon] train, or any signs of permanent possession by the white man excites bitter hostility. It is their last hope; if they yield and give up this, they will have to die or ever after be governed by the white man's laws; consequently they lose no opportunity to kill or steal from and harass the whites when they can do so. The game still clings to its favorite haunts, and the Indian must press upon the steps of the white man or lose all hope of independence."

She was absolutely right—but understanding the situation did not make her position as a victim of it any easier to accept. The Indians were fighting because they wanted to keep on living in the way they were accustomed to living—by following the buffalo herds. They fought in defense of the vast lands where they lived and hunted.

Her captors kept her busy. One of her tasks was to prepare red willow bark for their pipes; they used it instead of tobacco. They liked her singing, so they made her sing while she worked. After she learned their language, she entertained them by translating stories from an old school reader that had been in her wagon.

On August 8, the Sioux rode out on the warpath again— and this time the battle was so close that Fanny could hear gunfire. She longed for rescue, but the tribe hurried her on and would not even let her turn around and look. The women and children hastened on all day without water, and children cried with thirst until they camped that night beside a river.

Two or three wounded warriors were brought into camp, and—for some reason she never understood—Fanny was ordered to care for them. She had not the faintest idea of how to treat wounds, but if the Indians thought she had some special skill at doctoring, she was willing to let them think so.

Pretending to be very wise, she succeeded in convincing them that she was a most useful doctor.

The soldiers kept pursuing, and the Indians continued to flee. Sometimes the warriors brought back bloody uniforms and fresh scalps as trophies. But this constant flight was very hard on the moving village—water was scarce in the Badlands, and their horses, without enough grass to eat, became weak. The frantic Sioux began to leave behind great quantities of their possessions, sometimes even tepees with all their contents.

By the time Sully's army stopped chasing them, the Indians who had been rich in horses and furs and the comforts of nomadic life were poor again, hungry and desperate. They were in mourning, too, for their dead, and they gashed their bodies with knives, cut off their hair, and blackened their faces.

Poor Fanny got the blame for all their troubles. She was called to a council and sternly informed that she had to die because her white brothers had killed so many of the Sioux.

But Chief Ottawa defended her. He said that Fanny was innocent; she had sung for the people and smiled at them, and the children loved her. So her life was saved, and the tribe moved slowly on, starving, trying to find better hunting grounds. When horses and dogs died of hunger, the people butchered them and ate the meat.

One day on this endless journey, an Indian rode up beside Fanny, and what she saw attached to his saddle gave her so frightful a shock that she fainted and fell off her horse. She saw a bright little shawl that had been Mary's, and a scalp with long, fair hair. For several days thereafter, Fanny was almost delirious with horror.

Weakened by that experience and by long hunger, she could not possibly do all the work expected of her by Ottawa's senior wife, and a family fight resulted. The old woman flew at her with a knife, Ottawa struck the old woman, and she stabbed him several times. The wife's brother fired his gun at Fanny but missed; the bullet broke the chief's arm near the shoulder. Fanny ran for her life but was captured and dragged back.

She never saw the bad-tempered older wife again and did not know what became of her. But Fanny nursed the chief, living in the tepee with the women of his family. When Ottawa's wounds festered, Fanny bathed and dressed them as well as she could, but he remained a cripple.

Bright hope dawned for Fanny Kelly when an Indian named Porcupine joined the Ogallalas and gave her a message from Captain Levi Marshall at Fort Laramie: Porcupine was to take her there and be rewarded. Her heart leaped with joy—but Porcupine had no intention of doing what he had promised. He casually informed her that when he returned to the fort he would report that she was dead.

Early in September, Fanny's captors attacked a military escort that was protecting a big wagon train. The Sioux killed twelve persons and captured two wagons loaded with whisky and other goods. The train "forted up" and, in this defensive formation, soldiers held off the Indians with howitzers.

Old Ottawa ordered Fanny to write a letter to the leader of the train, assuring him that the Indians wanted peace. This was a lie; the Indians planned to attack again as soon as the wagon train began to move on.

Fanny had experienced so much deceit that she thought she might try some tricks herself. She wrote the letter, all right, in English, translating from the Sioux language as old Ottawa dictated—and he counted every word she wrote. But she contrived, by joining some words together and condensing the information, to warn Captain Fisk of the plot and to beg for rescue.

Captain Fisk wrote back that he didn't trust the Indians, so Fanny had to write him another letter, assuring him of their friendship. She managed to get her own message into this one, too. After much pleading, she borrowed a pair of field glasses from the Indians and stood on a hill, watching the soldiers. They could see that a white woman was really there.

Later she learned that the men in the wagon train were all determined to fight for her release—one even offered eight hundred dollars to ransom her—but Fisk wisely refused to endanger them. The Indians' anger increased when they found and ate a box of crackers and several members of the tribe died. The crackers had been poisoned with strychnine by someone in the train whose relatives had been massacred.

Day after day, negotiations for the rescue of Fanny continued, but the Indians would not sell her at any price. At last Fisk and his party gave up the attempt and went on—but he spread the word that Mrs. Fanny Kelly was with the Ogallala Sioux.

A delegation of the Blackfeet Sioux (not the Blackfeet tribe, but a branch of the Sioux tribe) went to Fort Sully (near present Pierre, South Dakota) to ask General Sully for a peace treaty. He refused, telling them that their white woman captive must be returned before any treaty could be made. They must get her from the Ogallalas and bring her to the fort. Then they could have peace and a fine reward as well.

Leaders of the Blackfeet and the Ogallalas spent two days in council, discussing the offer. The Ogallalas refused to give up the captive of whom they were so proud.

"Very well," the Blackfeet suggested, "let us use her as a decoy. Give the white woman to us, and we will take her to the fort. When the gates are opened to let us take her in, we will atack and wipe out all the white solders."

Fanny was horrified at the plot, but she was helpless. She was handed over to the Blackfeet Sioux, who took her 150 miles to their own village. She suffered terribly from exposure on the way.

She made a fearful decision. She would warn Fort Sully even if it meant her death. She sent a letter to the fort by a friendly Indian named Jumping Bear.

Early in December, 1864, more than a thousand warriors rode with Fanny to the fort. Actually, she walked most of the way to keep from freezing. On December 12, eight chiefs went up to the gates of the stockade with the rest following, singing and chanting.

Fanny did her poor best to freshen up before meeting white men again. Long before, she had narrowly escaped being tattooed by pretending to faint, but she had to wear the same face paint that the Indian women did. By rubbing snow on her face, she managed to get most of the paint off before the officers rode out from the fort. They greeted the chiefs and the trembling captive and escorted them inside. Then the gates were hastily closed—and Fanny was safe.

She couldn't believe it. She asked feebly, "Am I free, indeed free?" She was.

She had been a captive for more than five months. Three women at the fort did everything they could for her comfort, and the post doctor cared for her—she was badly frozen. The whites told her that her eyes wore a strange, wild expression, as if she were in constant dread.

One day there was great commotion. The mail had arrived in a wagon that was sometimes used as an ambulance. This was a great event at the isolated post. Very soon a soldier approached Fanny and said, "Mrs. Kelly, I have news for you. Your husband is in the ambulance!"

She was so overcome that she could not show emotion. She walked numbly toward Josiah, and when he took her in his arms even the soldiers wept. His hair was sprinkled with gray now, and his face was pale, but she knew his voice.

From him she learned what had happened to little Mary. The child had succeeded in getting back to the road where wagon trains went. Three or four soldiers, on their way to Fort Laramie, had seen a small child standing on a distant bluff, holding out her hands for help, but they were sure she was a decoy put there by Indians lurking in the ravine between them. Just the same, the soldiers were going to risk crossing, but a party of Indians came into sight. The soldiers fled to a small fort, where Josiah Kelly arrived soon afterward. He begged the officers there to give him a detail of soldiers to search for the child, but the danger was so great that for two days they refused. Then he set out—and found Mary's body, scalped and pierced with three arrows. He buried her there.

Kelly had done everything humanly possible to rescue his wife. Two companies of soldiers, alerted by a telegraphic message to Fort Laramie, had set out in pursuit but could not catch up with the Sioux war party. Kelly offered a reward of nineteen horses to any Indian who would bring Fanny back. Some Indians did bring in a white woman and her child, assuming that any white woman would do, but the woman was not Josiah's young wife.

Kelly sent many Indian messengers to look for Fanny. Some of them actually talked to her—but they came back and said they could not find her. He paid some of them as much as four hundred dollars in trade goods. He was in Kansas, trying to raise a company of volunteers to rescue her, when he learned from his brother, an army general, that she was safe at Fort Sully.

Fanny was in the post hospital for almost two months, undergoing treatment for her frozen hands, feet, and face.

In the summer of 1865, the Kellys went to Fort Ellsworth, Kansas, where they built and operated a hotel. In July, 1867, during a cholera epidemic, Josiah died. Fanny was pregnant. She gave birth to a son and, two or three years later, having sold the hotel, she moved to Wyoming to live with some survivors of the massacre in which she had been taken captive. This was probably the Larimer family.

There she wrote a book about her experiences, and soon afterward she went to Washington, D.C., to try to get a settlement from the Government for her services in warning the military escort of the wagon train that she had kept from destruction and the officers at Fort Sully about the treachery planned by the Sioux. Later she did receive a reward of five thousand dollars for this.

But while she was in the East on this errand, a book was published that made her furious. It was called *The Capture and Escape; or Life Among the Sioux*, and the author was Sarah L. Larimer, who announced that in her second book she would tell about Fanny Kelly's experiences.

Fanny claimed that her own manuscript had been stolen. She must have taken angry legal action of some kind, because Mrs. Larimer's second book never appeared. Fanny Kelly's own *Narrative of My Captivity Among the Sioux Indians* was published in 1871.

Mrs. Kelly married a man named Gordon in 1880 and died in 1904, when she was fifty-nine years old.

*   *   *

Some other girls who were captured by Indians and then rescued were the daughters of John German.

While the frontier was still untamed, many single men went west for adventure (which wasn't hard to find), but men with families usually made the move because they hoped for more prosperity than they left behind them.

This was the case with John German, a Georgia farmer, who fought on the Southern side in the Civil War. He returned to his farm in 1865, in poor health because of the severe privations he had suffered as a prisoner of war, to find that guerilla troops had stolen most of the livestock. Sick at heart as well as in body, he resolved to take his wife and four children to Colorado to get a fresh start.

But times were hard, and the Germans could not scrape together enough money to buy even the basic necessities for the long journey. For five years they worked and saved and dreamed. Then they packed their belongings in a covered wagon and set forth, always with some members of the family walking because there wasn't room for all to ride. By that time, there were seven children—one boy and six girls.

They didn't get to Colorado. In Howell County, Missouri, they traded their wagon and oxen for a small homestead claim and settled down for a while. Even the children worked for wages when they could get jobs. Catherine, the third oldest, who was fourteen, earned fifty cents a week by doing housework all day for a neighbor.

They had settled in malaria country, and there was much sickness in the family, so they moved on to Kansas. On August 14, 1874, they set forth again for Colorado.

The family consisted of John German and his wife Lydia; Rebecca, twenty; Stephen, eighteen; Catherine, seventeen; Joanna, fifteen; Sophia, twelve; Julia, seven; and Nancy Adelaide, called Addie, who was five years old. Of these nine people, five had less than a month to live.

They had no warning of trouble ahead. They saw only a few cowboys or friendly Indians as they traveled. But the fear and anger that boiled among the hostile Indian tribes were an unseen menace. The buffalo herds on which the red men depended for everything that made life good were being mowed down by white men who sold only the hides and left the meat to rot.

On June 27, a very large war party attacked the old trading post of Adobe Walls, in Hutchison County, Texas, where hide hunters fought them off. (Cynthia Ann Parker's son Quanah was one of the Indian leaders in this battle.) Angered by defeat but not discouraged, some of the Cheyennes continued on the warpath.

About seven weeks after the Battle of Adobe Walls, the warpath led them to the German family's peaceful trail camp in western Kansas, not far from the Colorado border.

On the morning of September 11, the Germans broke their overnight camp, packed their belongings in the wagon, and began to move on. Catherine, seventeen, went to help her brother Stephen drive the livestock. Stephen, with his rifle in his hand, said, "There's an antelope—I'm going to shoot it."

At that moment a war party of fifteen Cheyennes swooped down from behind a hill.

Catherine tried to stay with her big brother, but the attackers caught and killed him, and she was struck in the thigh by an arrow. An Indian seized her, pulled out the arrow, mounted his horse while holding her tightly, and rode toward the wagon. Rebecca lay dead; she had tried to defend herself with an ax. Both parents were struck down and killed.

The Indians looked over their five young captives, snatching off the girls' sunbonnets to see whether they had long hair. Joanna, fifteen, did—so they shot her and took her scalp.

The remaining four sisters went through a long time of terror. They were treated with a strange mixture of decent kindness and savage cruelty. One of the two women with the war party—Catherine called her Little Squaw—was sometimes kind. The other, Big Squaw, delighted in keeping the girls hungry and scared.

With no explanation to the older girls, the two younger ones were taken away.

"They've killed our little sisters," Catherine whispered.

Twelve-year-old Sophie answered, "They're better off than we are."

The girls had no idea where they were being taken or what was going to happen to them. They were utterly miserable; they couldn't eat the half-raw buffalo and horse meat that the Indians enjoyed, so they went hungry. Once when Catherine was roasting a piece of liver on a stick over the campfire, Big Squaw snatched it away and ate it before she could get even a bite.

Often the men threatened to kill their captives. Catherine reached the point where she didn't really care any more and she let the Indians know it. After that they treated her better, assuming that she was very brave instead of scared to numbness.

The Indians traveled fast, with much confusion, plainly worried about being pursued, but the girls didn't find out who the pursuers were. Sometimes even the Indians had only one meal a day because they did not dare stop in their frantic flight.

In spite of her terror, Catherine kept a daily journal for the first two weeks, writing in a small notebook with the stub of a pencil. But she lost both and after that had a hard time keepings track of the days that passed.

When the raiders got ready to make their triumphal entry into the camp of their people, Catherine and Sophia saw with horror that the long-haired scalps of their mother and their sister Rebecca had been divided into five pieces to show how many persons in the family had been killed. Holding these pieces on long sticks, the war party raced their horses through the village, yelling and firing guns. Both men and women grabbed at the girls as their horses pounded by, and Catherine's dress skirt was torn to shreds.

Catherine and Sophia were taken into separate Indian families and seldom saw each other. Catherine's foster mother treated her with alternate kindness and cruelty, going into sudden rages and striking the girl or throwing things at her.

The two older sisters were with a village of about three hundred lodges on the Staked Plains in Texas. Each lodge, or tepee, was the home of as many as ten persons.

Catherine's Indian mother gave her a new buffalo robe for her bed on the ground and a blanket for it as well. The girl was grateful to be able to sleep warmly. She even had a small pillow, which her Indian father had found and given her.

The food sickened her. It was always meat, only slightly cooked in hot water, and there was seldom any salt. Her Indian parents gave her a frying pan and a broken knife and let her cook her own food, but Sophia, who was with another family, didn't have this privilege.

Both girls at last got new dresses to replace their torn and filthy clothing. These Indian dresses were made of straight pieces of cotton cloth sewed down the sides, with a hole at the top for the head, and crude, straight sleeves, not sewed together underneath. Catherine also had a man's shirt to wear under the dress for warmth, and each girl wore a blanket. Even well-dressed white women wore shawls, so a blanket was not very much different. The girls wore moccasins. Their shoes had been taken away from them because the Indians thought they might leave tracks that could be identified by white pursuers.

There were never any clean clothes. There was never a bath, and there was no soap. The girls seldom had a chance to comb their hair.

Grieving for the five family members she knew were dead, and frantic with worry about her surviving sisters (and for her own future), Catherine did her humble best to understand the savages with whom she had to live. She learned Cheyenne from her foster parents' young son and taught him English. Her sister Sophia did not have Catherine's mature attitude; Sophia refused to learn the Cheyenne language or to do anything but mourn.

Catherine tried to please her foster mother by bringing wood and water to the lodge without being told, but this only made the woman cross and bad tempered. One evening the discouraged girl failed to set out voluntarily to do these chores. The Indian woman, whose language the girl was beginning to understand, said very kindly, "White girl go get water."

Her sudden change of attitude made Catherine realize that she was wrong in doing work without being told. Her foster mother wanted the satisfaction of ordering her around to show who was boss! Catherine was called "Ve-ho-ka," meaning Young White Girl.

Sophia was taken to another lodge, and the older sister could not find her. Later Catherine learned that Sophia was with Chief Grey Beard's band, which had left the main village.

The Indians kept on moving. When they camped, Catherine considered it a blessing to have work to keep her hands busy. She did everything she could to co-operate with her captors and earn their approval. The women gave her beads to string, using buffalo sinew for thread in a bone needle. She earned the good will of some of the men by making their simple shirts with button holes and bone buttons—the Indian women simply used sticks and string for fastening. Catherine helped the young women trim their dresses with strips of bright cloth. They paid her back in friendly fashion by chopping some of the wood that she had to collect for the lodge fire and helping her to her feet when she could not rise with the load.

Every few days the whole camp moved, with much excitement and yelling, because white soldiers were on the Indians' trail. One day when the move was very sudden, Catherine's Indian mother, Wasati, told her so many things to do all at once that the girl forgot to fasten her saddle girth securely, and she fell off the horse, saddle and all. Wasati became so angry that she snatched a rope, doubled it, and whipped Catherine, but Wasati's old mother wiped the tears away with her dirty sleeve and told the girl kindly to hurry. Catherine noticed, when they all rode off, that they were leaving many of their belongings in their hasty departure.

She began to have strange dreams at night. Once she saw her dead brother Stephen and tried to follow him. Still asleep, she rolled into the fire and burned a big hole in her good buffalo robe. Her Indian parents were angry, but the dream cheered her all the next day.

That night she dreamed that her mother came and kissed her and said, "Catherine, do the very best you can." For the rest of her life, that memory was a comfort to her, even when she was an old lady. It's good advice in almost any situation: Do the very best you can.

Again, dreaming, she rolled into the campfire and burned more holes in her bedding. Wasati told her she would have to sleep out in the cold, and she was perfectly miserable.

She had a frightening experience while sleeping outside the lodge—a man picked her up and started to run off with her. Catherine was seventeen, and Wasati wanted her to get married, but the girl had absolutely refused. According to custom, however, a couple was considered married if the young man could carry off the girl to his lodge. Catherine kicked, bit, and scratched her captor, and after running with her about one hundred feet he put her down, remarking, "I will not take her while she fights!"

She never knew who the Indian was but she was always grateful to him for letting her go. After that, her Indian father drove stakes into the ground inside the tepee so that she couldn't roll into the fire, and she was allowed to sleep inside where she was safe.

Catherine believed (because she needed desperately to believe) that her dreams meant she would sometime be returned to her own people. She had more basis for hope after another band of Cheyennes joined those with whom she was traveling and she met Chief Stone Calf. He was friendly, and he knew a little English; she spoke a little Cheyenne, so they could talk.

Stone Calf said he was sorry that some of his people had committed a crime against her people, and he would try to have Catherine and Sophia returned to the whites.

The whole group of Indians began to travel east under Stone Calf's leadership.

The month was now December. Snow on the ground made it hard for the horses to find enough grass to eat, and they were weak from hard travel. When they died of starvation, the hungry Indians butchered them for meat. Later, Catherine learned that white soldiers were driving the Cheyennes hard, trying to starve them into submission and rescue the captive girls.

One day, working at her usual chore of carrying firewood, Catherine met Sophia—and at first did not recognize her.

Sophia, dressed like an Indian woman, had become so tanned by exposure that she looked Indian. It was almost three months since the older sisters had last parted. They cried for joy.

Sophia asked, "Have you seen Julia and Addie?"

"I dreamed of them last night," Catherine answered, "But I haven't seen them and I don't expect ever to see them again."

"They were alive a month or six weeks ago," Sophia assured her.

An Indian had taken Sophia to see some white captive children who had just been brought into the camp. Seven-year-old Julia was so weak from hunger that she could hardly sit up. Addie, who was five, was so thin that Sophia didn't recognize her.

The little girls had been through an experience that seems impossible to believe. Julia, who told the story, may have exaggerated unknowingly; after all, she was a very little girl. Their captors had left them behind, and the children wandered alone. At a deserted army camp they ate grains of corn scattered where horses and mules had been fed, and they picked up crackers and other scraps.

When this food was gone, they gathered wild plums, berries, and wild grapes, and ate tender stems and roots—whatever they could find. At night they trembled with fear because wolves prowled around them. At last some Indians found them.

Sophia was allowed to talk to the little girls for only a few minutes. Then she was dragged away, and when she told Catherine the story, she had no idea where the small sisters were.

Sometime after this, Chief Stone Calf sent for Catherine to come to his tepee with her Indian mother. He told her

that five men had gone to Fort Sill, in Indian Territory, to
arrange for the return of herself and Sophia to the United
States troops there! You can imagine her joy.

Four days later, the chief sent for her again. He handed
her a letter from General Nelson A. Miles telling her that
little Julia and Addie had been rescued on November 8,
1874. The general's letter was dated January 15, 1875.

She longed to keep the letter, but she had to give it back to
Stone Calf. Then she ran through the camp, searching for
Sophia. The two older sisters rejoiced together. From that
time on, they felt that they could endure any hardships, because they were full of hope.

Later, the older sisters found out how Julia and Addie had
been rescued. Major General Nelson A. Miles had learned
that some white girls were being held by Chief Grey Beard,
leader of a strong hostile band. Miles assigned Lieutenant
Frank D. Baldwin, chief of scouts, to command a detachment
convoying twenty-three mule teams with empty wagons to a
supply camp on the Washita River. Lieutenant Baldwin's
orders permitted him to decide whether to follow any Indian
trails he saw. If he came upon a large body of Indians, he was
to notify General Miles and either attack or pursue them, as
he saw fit.

All the soldiers were determined to rescue the captive girls.
They moved fast, the infantrymen riding in the wagons. The
morning of November 8, scouts rode out before daylight to
see whether any Indians were around, and a scout named
Schmalsle came back at breakneck speed to report a large
Indian camp. He had recognized Grey Beard's tepee by the
designs painted on it.

Lieutenant Baldwin decided to attack at once, although his
soldiers were outnumbered at least two to one. He sent
Schmalsle back to give this information to General Miles, but

he could not wait for reinforcements. A bugle call signaled the attack, and the cavalrymen and wagonloads of foot soldiers all tore pell-mell down a hill into the Indian camp.

The Indian women and children ran in every direction while their men stood fast, firing to protect them. Then the Indian men fled, too. After a twelve-mile chase, the army's men, horses, and mules turned back, utterly exhausted. They had been fighting for four hours. They had defeated more than three hundred warriors.

In the deserted camp, they found Addie and Julia, too starved and weak to walk. The children were bruised and sunburned almost beyond recognition. Their hands were like birds' claws. Their scanty clothing was in rags.

The toughest, roughest soldiers in the rescue party were overcome with emotion at sight of the pitiful little girls. One teamster said, while tears ran down his cheeks, "I have driven my mules over these plains for three months, but I will stay forever or until we get them other girls."

It was the younger pair of sisters who told their rescuers that Catherine and Sophia had been captured at the same time they were. The soldiers cared for Addie and Julia tenderly and turned them over to James L. Powell, an Army doctor. General Miles had them photographed a few weeks after they were rescued.

The name of the German family has come down to us in books about the history of the West as Germaine. That was the way General Miles spelled it in his official reports. Even if Addie and Julia had known how to spell their last name, they were too sick to care.

Incidentally, Lieutenant Baldwin, whose decision to attack Grey Beard's camp had resulted in the rescue of the little girls, received a Congressional Medal of Honor (his second) for his bravery.

Even after the older girls had reason to hope they would be rescued, there was a long delay. Kiowa Indians, friendly to the whites, had been sent by the military authorities to persuade the hostile Cheyennes to bring the girls to Fort Sill. The Cheyennes, on the other hand, wanted to hand over their captives at another place, farther away. A valuable ransom would be paid for the girls' return, in any case.

Day after day, the Cheyennes and the two older German girls and the starving ponies of the tribe plodded through winter storms. One day in camp a Kiowa Indian came up to Catherine and spoke to her in English: "I have something for you."

From under his blanket he drew out a package. Catherine unwrapped it and found a photograph of Julia and Addie, the little sisters she had not seen since that terrible day in September.

On the back of it was pasted this message:

> Fort Sill, I.T.
> Jan. 21st, 1875
>
> To the
> Misses Germaine:
>   These Germaine sisters are well and are now with their friends. Do not be discouraged, efforts are being made for your benefit.
>
> Nelson A. Miles,
> Col. and Bvt. Maj. Gen.
> U.S. Army

She wanted to keep the picture, but the Kiowa took it back. Her Indian mother was very suspicious of him and told her not to talk to him because he was a bad man. Catherine certainly didn't think so.

The Indians continued to move northeast, crossing the

Texas Panhandle. They and their horses were so weak that they could no longer move fast.

On a day that Catherine never forgot, two white men came to the camp and she was allowed to talk to them. From them she learned what date it was: February 14, 1875. They were from a small party consisting of soldiers and Arapaho Indians. They brought the captive girls a wonderful treat of fresh biscuits, coffee, and a tin can of tomatoes.

Whether both girls would actually be returned was still touch and go. Grey Beard, whose village had Sophia, did not want to let her go. She was very disconsolate, sure that she was going to be killed. Chief Stone Calf kept arguing but could not persuade the other leader. Finally he went to the Cheyenne agency without the rest of them.

Catherine was now having trouble with her Indian mother, who wanted to keep her but realized that she couldn't. Wasati sometimes treated the girl very badly, and then cried and kissed her because she was sorry.

February 27 was a great day. Chief Stone Calf and two white men, one of them a Mexican interpreter, came riding into camp in an army ambulance, a wagon drawn by mules. Catherine wanted to tell Sophia this exciting news but couldn't find her.

The next day was even more wonderful. Chief Stone Calf and Catherine's Indian father helped her into the ambulance, and they drove off to look for Sophia. She was not in the lodge with the family that owned her, but they caught up with her.

As the ambulance moved along, the driver had Catherine point out to him the Indians who had taken part in the massacre of her family. She identified sixteen of them. One more, the leader of the party, had gone to South Dakota.

At the Canadian River, the ambulance stopped. There a

wagon load of provisions was waiting, the ransom that would free the girls. The Indians were so hungry that they ate the food without bothering to cook it, but Sophia and Catherine had a very good meal provided by their driver.

Strangely enough, the Indian women gave a kind of farewell party in honor of the German girls, making a pile of buffalo robes and blankets to give them a seat of honor. Some of the older women cried—but the rescued captives didn't. Catherine and her sister were delighted to put on new, clean clothing sent by ladies at the Cheyenne military headquarters and to discard their worn and filthy Indian dresses.

Near evening on March 1, soldiers lined both sides of the road leading to the Cheyenne Agency, in Indian Territory, waving their caps in greeting and shouting a loud welcome to the rescued girls. Catherine and Sophia burst into tears of relief and joy. When they were taken into the commanding officer's tent, they were so overcome with emotion that they couldn't even thank him for arranging their rescue.

White women at the mission school were wonderfully good to the forlorn, hollow-eyed girls, with their uncombed hair and weather-darkened skin. Sophia, twelve and a half years old, weighed only sixty pounds. Catherine, almost eighteen, weighed eighty.

News of the two younger sisters was waiting: they were safe in the home of Mrs. Patrick Corney in Fort Leavenworth, Kansas. Catherine and Sophia rested and recovered their health at the mission school for three months. Sophia, who had refused to learn Cheyenne when she lived with people who spoke nothing else, learned Arapaho from the children in the school!

In June, arrangements were made for the two older girls to go to Fort Leavenworth, where they were reunited with the little sisters whom they had not seen for nine months.

The grandparents of the girls, back in Georgia, offered them a home, but Catherine decided that they should not accept it. The relatives were very poor, and the girls would have been a great financial burden to them.

Catherine was old enough to go to work and support herself. General Miles arranged for good homes for the other three girls and saw to it that twenty-five hundred dollars in money was appropriated for each of the four. This money came from funds that Congress had voted to pay for food and supplies for the Indians.

Catherine and Sophia had a "common school" education —that is, grade school. The younger girls graduated from high school, as very few girls did in those days. Julia attended a teachers' institute and earned a teaching certificate. Addie attended Kansas State University for two years.

All four girls married, had families, and lived to be old ladies. Addie had eleven children. On July 4, 1957, a monument to the German family was dedicated in the Fort Wallace (Kansas) Cemetery. Thirty sons and daughters of the German sisters were present, and so was Julia, ninety years old, the last survivor of her generation.

2

Some Were Dedicated

✌

Mary Richardson Walker and the Sisters of Providence

THE MISSIONARY SPIRIT was very strong in the 1830's. Americans in the eastern states were intensely conscious, through sermons they heard in church and reports from missionaries in the field, of the tremendous number of people in the world who had never heard of Christianity.

Many a young woman yearned to spread the gospel in far places, but no woman could go alone. The earliest Protestant ministers who ventured forth found that they could not be farmers (to support themselves) and preachers and still do their own housekeeping. They needed dedicated wives to free them of some of their labor.

The first white women to cross the Rocky Mountains were Narcissa, the beautiful blonde wife of Dr. Marcus Whitman, and Eliza, the plainer but equally dedicated wife of Henry Spalding. These women were both from New York State.

In the spring of 1836, the Whitmans and the Spaldings set out together as missionaries to the Indians in the distant land called Oregon. Narcissa was a bride. Eliza was an invalid, not yet recovered from a long illness.

Anna Maria Pittman left Boston in July, 1836, with some

other women who were to teach in mission schools. She went the long way around—by sailing ship around Cape Horn to Hawaii (then called the Sandwich Islands) and from there to Oregon. She married the Reverend Jason Lee and died June 26, 1838, soon after the birth of a baby.

In March of that same year an earnest young couple from Maine, Elkanah Walker and his wife Mary, set out for the Far Northwest overland, as the Whitman-Spalding party had gone.

Elkanah's courtship was entirely unromantic or else very romantic, depending on how you look at it. He proposed marriage to Mary Richardson, aged twenty-six, the day after he met her; she accepted; and they got acquainted during their engagement, which lasted almost a year. That's romantic enough.

There's no star dust in the rest of the picture, though. Elkanah was a stranger to the Richardson family. He went to meet Mary because he was going to be a missionary and he needed a wife. She longed to be a missionary but had been turned down because she was a woman and unmarried. The Missionary Board played Cupid to the extent of suggesting that Elkanah Walker get acquainted with Mary Richardson.

It all worked out, although Elkanah was so shy, a friend commented, that he was afraid to say Amen at the end of his prayers. He was six feet four inches tall and, when he met Mary, he was thirty-two years old. He had been a farmer and could not afford to go to school to prepare for the ministry until he was twenty-seven.

Mary, the second of eleven children, had always been interested in missions. She had a good education and a brilliant mind.

They were married March 5, 1838. Their bridal journey ended almost six months later, on August 29, when they ar-

rived at Wailatpu, Oregon, where the Whitmans were living
and working among the Indians.

The Walkers went first to Boston, then to New York by
steamer, then to Philadelphia by train, to Pittsburgh by
stagecoach, and to St. Louis by steamboat. That was only the
beginning of the journey.

Their companions on the overland trip, nearly two thousand miles by horseback, were three other newly married
couples, Cushing Eells and his wife Myra; Asa Smith and his
wife Sarah; W. H. Gray and his wife; and three single men.

Travel by land was easier than an interminable sea voy-
age. All they had to do was ride horseback for almost two
thousand miles and camp out every night! The baggage of
the entire party was limited to a load for one horse—about
140 pounds, including a tent. Each person took his own
things in a valise only two feet long.

Their retinue included horses and mules, twelve head of
cattle (including two fresh milch cows), and a light wagon
drawn by one horse. They packed 165 pounds of flour, 57
pounds of rice, 25 pounds of sugar, and some other staples
like pepper and salt, and their meat came from game shot by
the men as the party moved slowly westward.

Mary found out very soon that her husband was subject
to moods of melancholy and bad temper. She wrote in her
journal on April 11 that she wished he wouldn't embarrass
her by continual watchfulness. He was critical of everything
she did. Later she wrote wistfully, "Should feel much better
if Mr. W. would only treat me with some cordiality. It is so
hard to please him I almost despair of ever being able to." A
few days later: "Rode twenty-one miles without alighting.
Had a long bawl. Husband spoke so cross I could scarcely
bear it."

A less congenial group of people it would be hard to find.

Every one of them was brimming with good intentions, but they bickered about anything and everything. Mary noted that scarcely one of the party wasn't intolerable some of the time. The men didn't get along with one another. Gray wrote later that Walker had no self-confidence, no positive traits of mind, and was not at all suited to be a missionary. And Smith wrote that Gray was rash, inconsiderate, and bossy. They were all strong-minded, determined people—who else would go forth to the wilderness to preach to the savage Indians?—so it's no wonder there were disagreements among them.

The days and the miles dragged slowly by. On July 24, the party reached Soda Springs (Idaho), and Joe Meek, a celebrated mountain man they had recently met, ate some of the bread that the ladies baked. They had no oven but used a tin reflector in front of an open fire. It was the first bread he had tasted in nine years. He had lived during this time with the Indians, who did not make bread.

Three days later, at Fort Hall, Mary had a tooth pulled. She had suffered intensely with toothache during the journey.

On August 15, at Fort Boise, the travelers were delighted with the food available there—butter, turnips, pumpkins, and salmon. Their diet on the trail was very restricted.

Mountain travel was terrifying to them. After descending one steep slope, Mary was so relieved to have it over with that she almost fainted.

On August 29, they reached their destination: Wailatpu, the mission where the Whitmans greeted them with delight. But welcome was about all they had to offer. The resident missionaries had not known how many people were coming, if any, and had not made preparations to accommodate eight visitors.

1

The Cayuse Indians were delighted, too. They flocked in
and constantly peered through the windows. Mary wrote in
her diary, "They annoy me very much and I will teach them
better manners as soon as I can acquire language enough."

The first year was awful. The Whitmans' house was too
small for one family, but several had to crowd into it.

Walker and Eells went to Tshimakain, about twenty-five
miles northwest of the present city of Spokane, Washington,
to found a mission among the Spokane Indians. Walker
wrote to Mary, urging that she learn the Nez Percé language
and warning that she had better get along with Mrs. Whitman. It was hard for anybody to get along with high-strung
Narcissa Whitman, however. Mrs. Eells couldn't do it.
Neither could Elkanah Walker. When he was there, Mrs.
Whitman didn't mind letting him know that she detested his
habit of chewing tobacco.

They had to eat horse meat, which Mary Walker hated
worse than her husband's tobacco habit. Besides, she was
pregnant, and she longed for some privacy, but there was
none in that crowded household. She helped with the work,
making soap, dipping candles, washing and sewing.

Elkanah was away on a horseback trip to Fort Walla Walla
when his son Cyrus was born on December 7. Mary had the
comfort of a doctor during her confinement, as many frontier
women did not. Marcus Whitman was a physician as well as
a preacher.

The Walkers tried to study the Nez Percé language, but it
was a difficult undertaking. Their Indian tutor had lost his
teeth, so his pronunciation wasn't clear. The language had
no alphabet, and nobody had ever compiled a grammar or a
dictionary.

In March, the Walkers and the Eells moved to Tshimakain.
Mary had no cookstove in the nine years she lived there. She

cooked in the fireplace, with a tin oven for baking. The cabins were of logs, chinked with mud, and their roofs were of poles, grass, and dirt. When it rained, great drops of mud leaked through. For many months, the windows had no glass but were covered with cotton cloth.

Mary worked hard and constantly, but she wondered sadly whether what she was doing was any help to the cause of converting the heathen.

Elkanah Walker was a shy man and a stern man. He had sought out Mary Richardson not so much because he was looking for romance but because a missionary needed a wife. He demanded much from her, and he came to depend on her. When he was away from her, he wrote letters that are surely love letters, even if he didn't mention the word love. Here is part of one:

> How it is I cannot tell but I should like to see you very much. I guess my heart is sick to see little Cyrus. I want to see him bathed once more. . . .
>
> It does appear to me that I am losing ground in the language. Yesterday I undertook to talk and was as dumb as a beatle. . . . I am tired of keeping an old bachelor's hall. Things do not go to suit me; when I come in from work tired almost to death, I want someone to get me a good supper and let me take my ease, and when I am very tired in the morning, I want someone to get up and get breakfast and let me lay in bed and take my rest. More than all, I want my wife where I can have her company and to cheer me up when the "blue devils" chain me down. Kiss Cyrus for me many many times.

Mary said not a word in her reply about her own continuing hard work or how tired she was or how her sleep was broken by the baby's demands. Her husband needed reassurance, and she gave it in full measure:

I am not half as lonely as you for beside the good company of the family, I have the dear little son to cheer me and so I am not as sad as I used to be when you are gone. When I am tired I press the little quiet sleeper to my bosom and moisten his face with my kisses. . . .

I often imagine what a good supper I would get for you were I there. When you come home I will let you have some good rests in the morning and I won't call you lazy and will do all a cheerful wife can do to drive away melancholy. . . .

Your notion that you are losing ground in the language is I suppose not a serious one. When a blade first shoots we can almost see it grow, but when the plant gets large, we may watch it day after day and scarce perceive the least alteration.

In the fall of 1839, there was a good harvest of corn and pumpkins—Mary helped with the field work—and the Walkers added a room to their cabin, *with a floor*. Mary wrote in her diary, "Find it pleasant to have a floor to wash again." A dirt floor can be tramped down to smoothness, and it can even be swept, but you can't keep dirt out of the house when the floor itself is of earth.

It was not until September 16 that the Walkers received their first mail from home, the first letters from families and friends since they had started west nineteen months before. The letters were read over and over—they were a tie with all that had been left behind.

Mary kept busy. She collected enough wild goose and duck feathers to fill a tick and make a feather bed, one of the civilized comforts that they had missed. She cooked and sewed and washed and looked after the baby, did the milking, worked in the garden—and reproached herself for not doing anything important for the Indians, whom she deeply pitied.

One day she dipped sixteen dozen tallow candles. In those days candles were not just something to make a dinner table look pretty. They were the only kind of illumination that pioneer settlers had, in addition to an open fire. Like many other necessities, candles couldn't be bought because there were no stores, so each housewife made her own.

Dipping candles was a tedious, time-consuming job. First, mutton and beef fat were boiled for several hours with some lye. After this mixture cooled, the impurities were skimmed and scraped off, and then the process was repeated for two or three days. Widely separated wicks—string or twisted fiber— were tied to dangle from a frame, and these wicks were dipped in the melted tallow. After the coating cooled, this had to be repeated over and over until the candles were as thick as desired.

Late in November the missionaries had compiled an alphabet for the Nez Percé language and were able to give some of the Indians their first reading lesson. Their school opened with thirty pupils. All along, they had held regular religious services.

On May 24, 1840, Mary woke about four, got up at five, helped with the milking, and before eight o'clock had an eight-pound baby girl, who was named Abigail.

When the Eells's house burned, they had to move in with the Walkers for a while. It was a good thing the two families were neighbors. The men were often away on long horseback trips in connection with the work of the mission, leaving the two women and their several children alone except for the Indians who lived in the area. Dr. Whitman couldn't always get there when a baby was to be born.

Along with her own housework and the care of her children, Mary Walker often had to nurse Myra Eells, who suffered many illnesses. Because of the continuing invalidism of

Mrs. Eells, Mrs. Walker always tried to catch up with her own work before she went to bed to have a baby.

One morning in March, 1842, she got up at five, had her housework done by nine, baked six loaves of bread, and put some suet pudding on to boil. At nine o'clock that evening, her third child was born. Dr. Whitman got there in time.

On November 29, 1847, the Cayuse Indians attacked the mission at Wailatpu and brutally murdered Marcus Whitman, his wife Narcissa, and eleven other persons who were with them there. Nobody knows for sure why the Indians, for whom the Whitmans had sacrificed the comforts of civilization, turned against them so horribly. There were rumors that the Indians thought the doctor was poisoning them.

They were, indeed, dying like flies, from a measles epidemic. This disease, not usually serious to white people, was often fatal to people who had no immunity to it. Dr. Whitman did his best for the sick; the sick died; therefore he must have killed them.

The two families at Tshimakain had plenty to worry about when news of the massacre reached them. The Spokane Indians were alarmed for their safety. Big Head, a Spokane chief, promised that his people would defend them, but warned that they must be very careful.

The obviously advisable thing for the Walkers and the Eellses to do was to flee to some safer refuge, because the hostile Cayuses were only 180 miles away. But Mary now had five small children and expected another in a month. Under those conditions, she could not face travel in winter. So they stayed, and went on hearing about Indian troubles. The tribes were fighting among themselves.

On December 31, 1847, Mary Walker bore her sixth child, a nine-pound boy. In March, Walker and Eells took their families to Fort Colville, a Hudson's Bay Company fur trading post. They would never again live at Tshimakain, which had been their home for nine years. Their missionary work was ended.

In June the Walkers went to Oregon City and rented a house with no furniture. They did not stay there long but moved to Forest Grove, where Elkanah Walker took up farming. He continued to preach at church services. He also continued to have spells of dyspepsia during which nobody could get along with him. He called these attacks his "blue devils." He suffered from stomach ulcers for most of his life. As his digestion grew worse, so did his disposition.

On a day in May, 1852, Mary Walker cooked breakfast and noon dinner and, about sunset, had her eighth and last child. Altogether, she had seven sons and a daughter.

In 1871, thirty-three years after the Walkers had left Maine, they returned for a visit. Many relatives and friends were dead, but it was good to go home. They traveled more comfortably this time, by ship to San Francisco, and across the continent on the Union Pacific Railroad, which had been completed two years before.

Their purpose in making the trip was to attend their son Elkanah's graduation exercises at the Bangor Theological Seminary. He became a missionary to China.

While the Walkers were in the East, they heard of a terrible fire in Chicago; it is known to history as the Great Chicago Fire. On the way home they visited a cousin in Chicago and saw some of the damage.

Six years passed, with Elkanah's health growing worse. He died in November, 1877, probably of cancer. His last words were, "His loving kindness."

A few weeks later, Mary wrote in her diary: "It seems as though I can't live without my husband. It is lonely to be a widow. I feel so lonely. Think so many things I want to tell

Mr. Walker. I realize more and more how much more I loved him than any one else."

Mary Walker, with her children grown and married, had time now to teach a Bible class, time to attend lectures, time to sit and talk to friends and neighbors—time to remember. For many years she took boarders.

In 1888, she journeyed to Whitman College, named for Marcus and Narcissa Whitman, to observe the fiftieth anniversary of the arrival of her party of missionaries in the Oregon Country.

In her later years, her once brilliant mind became dull and clouded with age. She died in December, 1897, aged eighty-three years and eight months. Surviving were five sons and a daughter, twenty-five grandchildren, and six great-grandchildren.

*   *   *

Among the other dedicated women who went west were several groups of nuns who braved the perils of travel to the Oregon Country to work among both Indians and white families. The "white" families, at first, were part Indian, because *voyageurs*—hardy, wandering French Canadian employees of the great Hudson's Bay Company—married Indian women.

The Oregon Country was a huge area, spreading from the Pacific Ocean to the Rocky Mountains, and extending from the northern border of California far up into Canada. In 1811, an American fur trader, John Jacob Astor, established a trading fort called Astoria at the mouth of the Columbia River. British traders explored the country and traded with the Indians for furs. For several decades, the United States—which was very far away—argued with the British Government about boundaries. So many American settlers emigrated to the Oregon Country that in 1846 the two nations signed the Oregon Treaty, by which some of the area became part of Canada and some became Oregon Territory.

The earliest settlers were American, British, and French; they were both Catholic and Protestant. All of them needed schools and hospitals. As late as 1850, the whole of Oregon Territory had only three public schools and twenty-nine private and denominational schools.

In 1844, six Sisters of Notre Dame de Namur traveled all the way from Belgium to the Willamette Valley to work among the Indians. They went by ship, across the Atlantic Ocean, down the east coast of South America, around Cape Horn, and north along the west coast of South and North America. Before them, in 1838, two priests, Father F. N. Blanchet and Father Modeste Demers, had reached the Oregon country by a different route. Fathers Blanchet and Demers went from Montreal clear across Canada by the overland route, traveling by boat and on horseback.

Five Sisters of Charity of Providence went to Oregon from Montreal in 1852, but both groups of nuns had to return to San Francisco. Times were bad in Oregon. For several years after the Whitman massacre, anti-Catholic feeling was bitter. In addition, the California gold rush took many settlers out of Oregon, and most of the newcomers from the East were Protestants.

In 1856, another group of five nuns from Montreal went by ship to Fort Vancouver, in the Oregon country. Their ship waited in New York a few days so as to carry the news of the 1856 national elections. (Democrat James Buchanan defeated Republican John C. Fremont for the Presidency.)

These intrepid Sisters, two of them very young (one was only eighteen), suffered terribly from seasickness, but their journey was shorter than their predecessors'. The year before, a railroad had been built across the Isthmus of Panama, so they crossed in comparative comfort—forty-seven miles in five hours—and avoided the tedious and dangerous sea journey clear around South America.

In what is now the state of Washington, they labored and built, started schools, cared for orphans and aged people, and established a hospital.

Four more Sisters of Providence left the Mother House in Montreal in 1864, spent some time in the Vancouver community and at Walla Walla, and on September 17 undertook a difficult journey to the east across several ranges of mountains to the St. Ignatius Mission in western Montana.

Their superior was Sister Mary of the Infant Jesus, aged thirty-four—the only one of the group who was over twenty-one. With them went three priests and two laymen whose job it was to get a big prairie schooner through country where roads were virtually nonexistent.

The party traveled for a whole month, the Sisters riding horseback as the men did, and sleeping on the ground with their saddles for pillows. One nun was kicked hard by her horse as she started to mount, but she kept up with the others in spite of her pain. Sometimes their food was gritty with wind-blown sand, and they had to struggle to keep their tents from blowing away. There were steep ascents, fallen timber, streams to ford. They prayed and sang and chatted as they rode.

These were the first white women to cross the Coeur d'Alene Mountains. On October 15, they reached the little settlement of Frenchtown, in Montana, after four hundred miles of travel. There was a small log church there, and a community with several Catholic families.

They had been meeting prospectors and gold miners who

warned earnestly, "You can't possibly live in St. Ignatius. No white woman could." But on October 17 they arrived, and they certainly could and did live there.

The priests had established a mission at St. Ignatius for the Indians in 1854 and had built a log chapel, two small houses, a blacksmith shop, and a carpenter shop. There was a flour mill, too, and a crude sawmill that cut logs into boards.

The priests had been teaching the Indian children, but they had discovered that day schools didn't accomplish very much. The Sisters' assignment was to establish a boarding school where little girls could live and learn and still be near their families.

Sister Mary of the Infant Jesus and her young nuns found their school building not yet finished, so they moved into temporary quarters, rolled up their sleeves, and began to sweep, scrub, and wash.

When the school was ready, they taught reading, writing, spelling, and simple arithmetic. Some of them also taught the English language, but one or two of them never learned it. Their native tongue was French, and they had to learn Salish, the Indians' language, before they could teach anything.

In the whole of Montana Territory at that time there were only about fifteen thousand white persons, and most of them were men without women. A few, however, had families with children who needed to go to school. The Sisters, therefore, opened a boarding school for girls and published this advertisement in the Territory's first newspaper, *The Montana Post,* at Virginia City, then a thriving gold camp:

Academy of the Holy Family,
For Young Ladies,
St. Ignatius Mission, M.T.

This Academy is under the direction of the Sisters of Charity. They will teach to read and write, Grammar and English Composition, Arithmetic, Geography, History, and the French language, if required. Sewing, and whatever is understood under the extensive word of Housewifery. Children must be provided with bed-clothing, two dresses for week days and one for Sundays, half a dozen pocket handkerchiefs, three towels, combs and basin, spoon, fork and knife. They will buy their school books in the Academy. For the sake of uniformity and good order, all the pupils will assist at the religious exercises of the Institution. All letters either sent or received, by the pupils, will be subject to the inspection of the Superiors. No visitor admitted without a written order of the respective parents or guardians of the pupil.

TERMS—Cash, and invariably five months in advance. Entrance Fee, $5.00; Board and Tuition, $25.00 per month; Washing and Ironing, $5.00 per year. The annual session will commence on the first of September, and end on the first of June. For further information, address

Rev. MOTHER MARY, (of the Infant Jesus) Superioress, or Rev. U. Grassi, S.J., Sup't St. Ignatius Mission, 36 miles North of Hellgate, Montana Territory.

What an embarrassing address for a religious school—"36 miles North of Hellgate"! That was the name of a pioneer community, however, and it is still the name of a canyon at the edge of the present city of Missoula. St. Ignatius is still a mission on the Flathead Indian Reservation, in the broad, beautiful Mission Valley, bounded at one edge by the awesome Mission Range of the Rockies.

The mission, like the Indians it served, was sometimes a victim of the greediness of Indian agents employed by the United States Government. In bitter cold weather, the priests asked the Government for clothing for the children, who were Government wards. They received two bolts of cotton print and two of unbleached muslin—useful, but not very warm—and three years later learned that the Indian agent had billed the Government no less than $1,600.66 for those four bolts of cotton cloth!

Some of the mission's supplies came up the Missouri River by steamboat from St. Louis to Fort Benton. The steamboat men transported this freight for the mission without charge. Then it was hauled by wagon for several hundred miles. On one occasion, the mission's only wagon was broken down and the brother who could have repaired it was sick, so the priests asked the Indian agent to lend them two government wagons that were not being used. The man who went to get them, to start for Fort Benton, found them already loaded, and since he had nothing to haul on that part of the trip, he took them, at the agent's request, to Deer Lodge, which was not out of his way.

Later the priests were shocked to learn that those wagons had hauled flour, ground at the Agency for the Indians, made from wheat that the Government had bought for the Indians. The agent had sold it in Deer Lodge for his own profit, pleased to have it hauled by Mission oxen and driven by a brother to make the theft look honest!

The Sisters continued to work at St. Ignatius. In 1872, Mother Caron came out from Montreal to report on their activities, broke her arm, and had to stay all winter. Soon after Easter she went to Missoula (a growing town that was becoming more important than Hellgate), taking Mother Mary of the Infant Jesus and Sister Mary Edward. In Missoula they established St. Patrick Hospital. The nuns moved into a house full of spider webs, with two small boxes as furniture.

Thirteen years later, the Order extended its hospital work

to Fort Benton. In 1892, it founded Columbus Hospital in Great Falls. It founded the College of Great Falls in 1932, and it conducts a children's home in the same city, Sacred Heart Academy in Missoula, and grade schools in Great Falls, Missoula, and Glasgow.

And what of the four Sisters who went to St. Ignatius, where they were told they couldn't possibly live? Sister Paul Miki died there in 1880, after sixteen years of devoted labor. Sister Remi sacrificed her health to her work and was recalled to Montreal for medical treatment. She died there in 1885, soon after arriving. Sister Mary Edward returned to the Mother House later. Mother Mary of the Infant Jesus lived for many years in Missoula and died there in 1917.

On August 26, 1964, at St. Ignatius, the Sisters of Charity of Providence celebrated the centennial of the arrival of the first four members of their Order. After a hundred years, the Order still runs a hospital—a new, modern one now—in the little town where, the first nuns were warned, white women couldn't possibly live.

The Superior of the Holy Family Hospital at the time of the centennial celebration was Sister Joseph Arthur, who had nursed Mother Mary of the Infant Jesus on her deathbed.

3

Some Came to Work—and Marry

Mercer's Belles

IN THE EARLY SPRING of 1864, Asa Mercer of Seattle made a speech in Mechanics' Hall in Lowell, Massachusetts, that influenced the lives of many eastern women and western men.

Mercer recommended an astonishing idea: that women from the east coast should go west to seek their fortunes. The young, busy town of Seattle needed them. Women could teach school there or give music lessons or work at a variety of ladylike jobs. He admitted that Seattle was crude and rough, but it wasn't *too* crude and rough. It needed the gentle influence of respectable, well-educated women. The Northwest was a land of plenty and of opportunity.

His audience listened attentively. Seattle sounded enticingly different from the industrial East! Lowell had forty thousand people depending on cotton mills for their livelihood, but the Civil War was in progress and no raw cotton was coming from the South. Unemployment was a terrible problem, even for men with families, and opportunities for women were more severely limited.

Another problem that Mercer didn't have to mention was that New England was plagued by a scarcity of young men and an overabundance of young women who wanted to get married.

Mercer didn't hold out to his audience the obvious advantages for marriageable young women in the Seattle area which swarmed with marriageable young men. It wasn't necessary. The young women figured it out for themselves. The whole thing was kept on a high level: when ten young ladies, ranging from fifteen to twenty-five, set forth some weeks later, they weren't hunting husbands; they were seeking jobs.

Asa Mercer offered comfortable accommodations for women for one hundred and fifty dollars for the trip, half price for children. This was a bargain. Passage safe and suitable for women normally cost twice that much. The fare covered passage by ship to the Isthmus of Panama, which had to be crossed, and then by another ship north to Washington territory.

Mercer set up a lot of rules, but the passengers didn't follow all of them. Men unaccompanied by their families were not welcome, but some went along anyway. Each passenger could take 150 pounds of freight. Daniel Pearson and two of his daughters went along, and Pearson made money in an ingenious way. Some of the unattached men didn't need to take their full allowance of 150 pounds, so he arranged to pack their trunks with shoes that he bought in Boston for two or three dollars a pair. He sold these in Seattle for ten to twenty dollars—a nice profit!

The journey was long and difficult, but it was a real adventure. From San Francisco, the group went north on a sailing ship that had brought lumber down the coast. There was a big reception in Seattle for the immigrants. Seattle's few housewives heartily welcomed the newcomer ladies, who all got jobs teaching school. All of them married except one, and she must really have wanted to stay single.

In less than a year, Mercer went east again to recruit a much larger party of women, this time specifically for wives. He planned to charge the women a fee, which would be paid by their husbands after they married. This time Mercer had serious problems. He was deep in debt, and he could not get the financial backing that he needed. Late in January of 1866 he gathered his passengers on the steamship *Continental*, which he had chartered. The ship would go clear around the southern tip of South America.

Mercer had planned to take seven hundred passengers, but he was able to round up only about one hundred, and only thirty-six of these were unmarried women.

The food was awful. For seventeen days in a row, one of the women recalled later, the main dish was undercooked beans. The ship's captain had all kinds of delicacies on his table, and you may be sure that the hungry passengers noticed. One woman got permission to go into the galley and bake a sheet of gingerbread, of which each passenger had a tiny bit. Another woman opened up a can of strawberry preserves so that everyone had a taste.

There was all kinds of friction on the ship. After the captain ordered his officers to keep away from the women passengers, one plain-spoken spinster tried to get even. She drew a chalk mark across the deck by the door of the "saloon," or lounge, and wrote, "Officers not allowed aft." The captain was so angry that he had her locked in her cabin as punishment.

During the long journey, the passengers amused themselves in various ways. There was much piano playing and group singing, various people gave readings and recitations, and the women knit vast quantities of yarn that Mercer had brought along. Much of the friction concerned Mercer himself. He was altogether too bossy. He tried to keep his ladies from playing cards or flirting with the ship's officers, and he even tried to make them go to bed at ten o'clock.

On February 3, the ship crossed the equator. A week later, it was off Rio de Janeiro, and naturally the passengers wanted to see this foreign city. Mercer tried to talk them out of it, warning that cholera and smallpox were epidemic, but in the week the ship was there, most of the women managed to go ashore and see the sights, with the enthusiastic help of the men on the ship. When they got around to the west side of South America, they visited a Peruvian port, too.

On April 24, the ship passed through the Golden Gate and dropped anchor in San Francisco Bay. It took a lot of policemen to keep the men of the city away from "Mercer's belles." Single men wanted wives, and married men had orders from their wives to bring back houseworkers. Twenty of Mercer's belles did stay in San Francisco.

All kinds of rumors had spread in Seattle. People there had heard that seven hundred women were coming, and there wouldn't be room for them all, so five hundred would be shipped down to Oregon. This was nonsense, as rumors usually are.

Some funny things happened. Several Seattle bachelors had signed contracts promising to pay Mercer three hundred dollars each for wives, and one young man had asked for a specific girl from back home. She hadn't come, but another girl by the same name had, from another state. The young man introduced himself to her: "I'm the feller that sent three hundred dollars by Mercer to bring you out for my wife. I suppose you're as willing to get married this afternoon as any other time, and I have to be home by sundown to milk the cows and feed the pigs."

The astonished young woman replied, "You're impertinent! I paid my own fare, and I won't marry you."

The puzzled and disappointed suitor answered, "If you didn't come to get married, what did you come for?"

"I came to do tailoring and earn my own living," she informed him, and sent him on his way.

A backwoods farmer came to town, looked over Mercer's belles, chose a widow with three small sons, proposed to the lady, and married her three hours later.

The group reached Seattle on May 29, and by June 9 there had been thirteen weddings. One of the bridegrooms was Asa Mercer himself, who married a passenger, Annie E. Stephens of Baltimore.

Mercer worked for many years for the advancement of the Northwest. Later he was a newspaper man in Texas for seven years; then he moved to Wyoming in 1883 and established a journal for livestock men. He wrote a famous book, *The Banditti of the Plains,* about a range war in Wyoming, and died August 10, 1917. He and Annie had three sons, two daughters, and many grandchildren.

The "Mercer Girls" helped civilize the Northwest. Almost all of them married, and their descendants have a right to boast of their pioneer great-grandmothers. One of Mercer's belles was asked, when she was an old lady, about her early years. She answered modestly, "I never did anything remarkable for Seattle, but I had eleven children, so I feel that I contributed to the population."

4

Some Were Protected

Harriet Sanders

We sometimes think of pioneer women as living in discomfort and danger and poverty, but this wasn't true of all of them. Harriet Fenn, who married Wilbur Fisk Sanders, shared his prosperity. She was protected and beloved, a devoted wife and mother, enjoying the good things of frontier life.

All the members of her family were great journal-keepers, and it is from their records of day-to-day occurrences that we know them, as well as from old newspaper stories. They were important people in early Montana.

Harriet was born April 25, 1834, in Tallmadge, Ohio; she was one week older than her husband, whose birthplace was Leon, New York. At twenty-two, he was admitted to the bar, and he practiced law for the rest of his life. During the early part of the Civil War he was acting assistant adjutant general on the staff of General James W. Forsyth, with the rank of colonel. He resigned his commission because of ill health and headed westward in 1863 with a wagon train including seventeen persons, most of them relatives.

Two of these emigrants were the Sanders' little boys,

Jimmy, not quite four, and Willie, almost two. All through this long camping trip, their mother kept a journal in which she recorded how far the wagons traveled each day, where the party camped, what she saw and did.

These travelers, way back in 1863, were by no means trail blazers. Thousands of families had preceded them. There were well-marked wagon trails—not roads, but easy to follow. There were guide books, which all the emigrant parties bought and studied. These books told where good water and feed for the stock could be found, warned of dangers to be avoided, and gave advice about fording rivers.

The members of the party were relatively prosperous. They could afford to buy whatever they needed for their journey, but careful planning was necessary. For instance, Harriet didn't pack enough salt, so she had to borrow during most of the trip. At the end of August, somewhere in the Rocky Mountains, the party came upon a whole acre of salt deposit several inches thick, and Harriet paid back her debt.

Why did the Sanders party go west? They weren't poor farmers looking for land so they could become prosperous. But westward was the direction that ambitious, energetic people *did* go, and back home in the United States the Civil War was raging.

Wilbur Sanders' uncle, Sidney Edgerton, about forty-five, had been appointed Chief Justice of the Supreme Court of Idaho Territory, so he *had* to go west. The rest went along because it was the land of promise.

They left Tallmadge, Ohio, on June 1 by railroad; at St. Joseph, Missouri, they took a boat for Omaha, Nebraska, and from there they set out in their covered wagons on June 16. Right away they had trouble, because the oxen they had bought to pull the wagons were young and skittish. The men in the party had to show the animals who was boss.

The women found that, in spite of their careful planning, everything they needed that first night of camping was in the bottom of the bottom box in every wagon.

Harriet Sanders had her share of difficulties, but she and the other women in the party also had a wonderful time. Back home, the labor of keeping house had filled their days, because the conveniences we expect now hadn't even been imagined yet. When you travel by wagon and camp every night, you have no house to keep! While the wagons moved, seldom more than fifteen miles a day, the women had more leisure than they had ever had before. They took full advantage of it, with clear consciences. Although they had all the problems of housekeeping-on-the-move, they also had time to relax, take naps in the moving wagons, and go for long sight-seeing walks. The train moved slowly, so they had no trouble catching up.

Wilbur's cousin, Lucia Darling, also kept a journal on this trip. There was plenty of time to observe and think and write. Lucia was one of the cooks. Hattie Sanders and Sidney Edgerton's wife, Mary, spent much of their time looking after the children. Mary's boy, named Sidney for his father, was a baby.

The women used small sheet-iron stoves for cooking. A normal breakfast included ham or bacon with biscuits or griddle cakes or both, plus gravy and plenty of milk. The party took along milch cows. Breakfast had to be hearty, because they couldn't be sure of stopping long enough to cook noon dinner.

Their camping places had to be chosen as much for the benefit of the stock as for the comfort of the emigrants. The cattle lived off the land, grazing on prairie grass. They needed rest and good water.

The dinner table had to be set up for each meal. It consisted of boards from the wagon propped across the mess box, and it was too high to reach if they sat on the ground. So they served themselves buffet style, and then found a place to sit, or else they stood up while eating.

Harriet Sanders was a great girl for looking on the bright side of things. On June 20 she wrote, "I certainly have enjoyed the journey so far much better than I had expected. This afternoon I rode the pony and carried Jimmie for an hour and then walked three miles. . . . The children are better than they were at home."

Three days later, while the wagon in which she was riding was crossing a river, the oxen stopped in quicksand. The men had to hitch on two more yoke of oxen to pull them out. Harriet was *very* glad when that was over! The same day, the party got word from some other travelers that there had been a big battle only twenty miles away—a band of Sioux Indians had defeated some Pawnees and United States troops.

The air was wonderfully clear, Harriet noted. She amused herself by seeing how many telegraph poles she could count without moving—118. During a terrible rainstorm, when she was snug in the wagon, she even admired the "grand lightning"—sheet after sheet of it. You can't stop lightning, so you might as well enjoy the spectacle.

One night she worried about her two little boys. Both were feverish and restless, and little Sidney Edgerton had the croup.

In their first thirteen days of travel, they covered 197 miles —a distance that requires about four hours now by car.

On June 30, a heavy rainstorm drove the Sanders family out of their wagon. Hattie and the boys took refuge in Aunt Mary's tent, which didn't leak so much as the canvas wagon top.

"There was no use crying," she wrote, "so we all went to

singing, and such a time as we had. Mr. Booth [one of the drivers] said that after that demonstration we need not be afraid of Indians—he knew they would run."

Eight days later they did have an Indian scare, and they did try singing as a defense. A few Indians approached at first, asked for food, and "behaved more mannerly" than Harriet had expected. But they came back with more Indians and demanded more food, which the men refused to give them. When the unwelcome visitors acted threatening, the whole party of travelers simply sat down, acting unafraid, and sang songs until the Indians left.

There is no mention of boredom in either Harriet's or Lucia's journal. Harriet had two active little boys to watch, in a country that contained such perils as rattlesnakes. She admired the scenery and picked wild flowers to press and send home. Altogether, the journey was restful as well as continually interesting.

Lucia, young and single, taking part in a great adventure, had more freedom than Harriet Sanders. More than once she stood guard all alone among the wagons during the night, watching for Indians! Once she had to stay up late anyway, making a bushel of "fried cakes"—doughnuts. Then she didn't have the heart to waken Sidney Edgerton, whose turn it was; he had gone to bed tired out from a long horseback ride. So she stayed up, ready to yell for help if trouble came. She wrote in her journal:

"The number of Indians and bears I saw on each side of camp among the willows in the moon light I did not count, but have decided today, in broad daylight, that it was all my imagination."

The women in the party were always on the lookout for suitable camp sites where they could catch up on the washing. There were no wash-and-wear garments in their time. Wet clothes would, of course, dry sometime—but not in a hurry. No man-made fibers had been invented. Clothing was made of cotton or wool, with linen for fine things. Sometimes Harriet Sanders pinned wet clothes to the canvas wagon top and let them dry as the wagon moved.

Ironing clothes was something that didn't have to be done while traveling in a wagon train, of course. Harriet starched sunbonnets and dried them into shape over pillows.

Sunbonnets, which took the place of hats, were pretty, practical, and easy to make. The deep brim (which had to be stiffened to make it stand out) shaded the face, the puffed back of the bonnet kept dust out of the hair, and a kind of skirt at the bottom kept the back of the neck from getting sunburned. The bonnet tied under the chin.

Changes in weather kept life interesting for everybody. On July 7, the sun was so hot that Harriet burned her fingers when she picked up tin pans to use in baking. Nine days later, the evening was so cold that everyone shivered, although the men were wearing coats and the women were bundled up in shawls.

A shawl was at that time the proper and fashionable outer garment for a woman, and it was a very handy wrap. It was square, smaller and of a softer weave than a blanket. Usually it had a fringe all around. Folded to a triangle and draped over the shoulders, it had to be pinned or held with one hand to keep it in place.

A shawl could be made or bought in almost any size or color, and it had the great advantage of fitting anyone who wore it. Besides being easy to drape gracefully on a woman when she wore it while walking, a shawl was also a carriage robe, and it was cozy for wrapping up a baby. Buggies and wagons were not only unheated; they were also open to the cold of winter.

It's plain, in reading these journals, that the women had more fun on the trip than the men did. The men (Lucia Darling always wrote "the gentlemen") had to figure out where to go next to find feed for the stock and water for everybody; they had to take care of the oxen's sore feet and mend wagons that broke down.

Very often the ladies of the party took long walks to get a closer view of spectacular cliffs and rocks. If *you* were walking toward some place seven or eight miles away, you would probably wear blue jeans, but in 1863 these dauntless hikers wore *hoop skirts*. It was proper for ladies to wear hoops, and these were proper ladies. Never mind how awkward it must have been to climb into a wagon a dozen times a day—*they wore hoops*.

Lucia and a few others went on one expedition that required wading across the Platte River. On the way back, so hard a storm struck them that they had to sit down on a sand bar to keep from being blown away. They were a deplorable sight when they got back to the wagons. Their clothing was drenched, their sunbonnets hung limply around their faces, and each of the women carried her hoops over one arm. Presumably with the other hand she tried to keep her soaked skirt from dragging, because the hoops weren't in there to hold it out of the mud.

In spite of Harriet's serene good nature, she did have worries. On August 16, Willie fell against the little stove, burning his hand badly. Harriet's husband, Wilbur, was sick, with a high fever and a terrible headache. She dosed him with Dover's Powder and a "blue pill." One of the oxen was sick, too. The men cured him with a large dose of bacon and vinegar.

On August 21, Harriet wrote with proper maternal pride, "Today is Willie's birthday. He is a little two-year old and a

SOME WERE PROTECTED   65

fine boy he is, if his mamma does say it. I little thought when
I left home that he would be so fat and healthy now. He
can run almost as fast as Jimmie."

Two days later, Wilbur felt better. He was able to eat a
grouse. Two weeks after that, his family almost drowned in
the swift Snake River. The party forded the river, and one
driver misunderstood which way he was to aim his team. All
the stock followed him, and Wilbur's wagon started to settle
in deep water. In it were his wife, the two little boys, a
friend named Amorette, and Lucia Darling. Wilbur leaped
out and went to the heads of the cattle and steered them in
the right direction. The passengers were pulled out, one by
one, by men on horseback.

Six days after that, on September 13, they had another
narrow escape. This time, Wilbur's wagon almost over-
turned on a narrow trail with a stream below. It was tipping,
with the inside wheels a foot off the ground, when the Chief
Justice of Idaho Territory leaped out and hung onto the
wagon until the other men could run up and help.

One thing that seems funny now is that these dauntless
pioneers weren't at all sure where they were going! Uncle
Sidney Edgerton was trying to reach the capital of Idaho Territory—but where was it? There was very little formal government in that vast area. Somewhere near Fort Laramie
(now in Wyoming), a traveler told the party that the capital
of Idaho was in Bannack. A day or two later, another man
said it was in Lewiston (now in Idaho). That's where it
really was, but Lewiston was often called West Bannack,
so it was easy enough for newcomers to become confused.

The problem of Uncle Sidney's destination was solved by
the difficulties of travel. On September 18, when the party
reached the Bannack that is now in Montana—sometimes
called East Bannack then—an early winter storm prevented

any more travel, so they settled down there for the winter.

Bannack, Montana, is a ghost town now, but in 1863 it was a roaring gold camp, consisting of rough cabins and tents strung out along Grasshopper Creek.

Little Jimmie Sanders, who had turned four years old during the journey, had been hearing his elders talk about Bannack so much that he expected it to be some kind of magnificent wonderland. But it wasn't much, after all, in his opinion.

He announced thoughtfully, "I fink Bangup is a humbug." And you may be sure that his loving mother wrote that bright saying in her journal!

The party stayed in "Bangup" that winter. There was no public school, so Lucia Darling set up a "subscription school" for the children of the settlement. No two pupils had the same textbooks; they had to use whatever their families had brought along.

Prices were high, because everything that anyone wanted— except gold, of course—had to be shipped in. Beef came in on the hoof, tough beef from oxen whose strength had been used up in hauling wagons. Gaunt and exhausted, they were slaughtered for their meat. In the fall of 1863, sugar sold for sixty cents a pound, raisins and potatoes for a dollar a pound. Eggs were a dollar and a half a dozen, and nobody guaranteed that they were fit to eat.

Wilbur Sanders entered the history of the West dramatically and heroically only three months after arriving in "Bangup." Harriet must have been both proud and worried when she learned of the events that took place in Nevada City, seventy miles away, one day in December.

The only law-enforcement officers in a very large area were Sheriff Henry Plummer and his deputies, who were members of an outlaw gang of robbers and murderers.

Society in these gold gulches was chaotic, for most of the men there had no intention of settling down to live. They had come to mine gold, not to help found a stable government. Each man looked out for himself as well as he could, and let everybody else do the same. Therefore the outlaws—known as road agents—prospered. There were more "good guys" than "bad guys," but the decent citizens were not organized, while the bad ones were, with the sheriff planning their holdups.

Nevertheless, three of the road agents were arrested—not by the sheriff, but by angry citizens—for a particularly brutal murder and tried in a miners' court. More than a thousand men attended the trial, which was held out of doors.

Any man who faced up to the road agents took his life in his hands, and Wilbur Fisk Sanders did exactly that. Happening to be in Nevada City on business, he consented to act as prosecuting attorney at the trial. One of the road agents, George Ives, was found guilty by a jury. But the crowd was excited, Ives' friends were stirring up more excitement, and he might still have gone free if no one had dared to follow through with a motion that he be executed.

Colonel Sanders had been in danger of death from the road agents' guns all during the long trial. (He knew it, and carried a loaded pistol in each pocket of his heavy coat. To let the crowd know he was armed, he "accidentally" fired one pistol right through his coat.) He endangered himself further by shouting the fateful words, "I move that he be hanged!"

Ives *was* hanged, then and there, in the cold moonlight. A few hours later the law-abiding men of the community formed a secret Committee of Vigilance that, within five or six weeks, hanged two dozen more evildoers and made the gulches safe for decent people.

Sidney Edgerton didn't have to find the capital of Idaho

Territory, after all. In 1864 Montana Territory was formed, the capital was Bannack, and Edgerton was appointed territorial governor by President Abraham Lincoln. He stayed in Bannack only a few months, because the newly formed territorial legislature asked him to go to the nation's capital to work for statehood for Montana.

Very soon Virginia City became the territorial capital instead of "Bangup," because rich new gold fields had been discovered along Alder Gulch, and twelve booming gold camps sprang up there. Virginia City was the biggest one. The Sanders family moved to Virginia City and found it an exciting place to live.

Mail was not delivered to the gold camps by the Government's postal system until the summer of 1864. Before that, privately operated "letter express" companies brought it, usually loaded on pack mules. The people in the camps gladly paid a dollar for each letter or newspaper received and seventy-five cents for each letter sent.

A newspaper, *The Montana Post,* began publication in Virginia City at the end of August, 1864. News from the outside world took a long while to get there, but at least people could find out what was going on right around them.

The newspaper announced, on September 17, that a new sheriff, Neil Howie, had been appointed by Governor Sidney Edgerton. Sheriff Howie was an honest man and a courageous one, as he had proved when he worked with the Vigilantes and as he was to prove several times in the future.

The same issue of the newspaper warned that the price of food would probably be very high during cold weather. Flour was being used up faster than it was being freighted into town. The wholesale price of Salt Lake City flour was $23.50 for one hundred pounds, and butter was a dollar a pound. The editor warned that during January, February,

and March, freight wagons wouldn't be able to get through
the mountains at all. He was right—but the hungry winter
lasted longer than three months that year. The freight wagons stopped coming at the beginning of December!

Almost all food came in wagons, pulled by oxen or mules
through the Rocky Mountains from Salt Lake City, more
than four hundred miles away. With snow drifts too deep for
travel, the freight wagons were stranded until spring. Their
drivers settled down to camp with their teams.

There wasn't enough flour in the gold camps to last
through the winter—and bread was one of the staple foods on
which everyone depended. Even under the most favorable
conditions, the variety of food was very limited. The territory
was so newly settled that there were few farms where even
potatoes could be raised in large quantities. These farms
were far from the mining camps, and the potatoes froze in
the wagons as slow-moving ox teams labored through the
snow. Beans and rice were also scarce—and no more of anything could come in until the snow melted.

Life in Virginia City was never dull. Two men, after an
argument over the huge sum of seven dollars and a half,
decided to fight a duel. A thousand people turned out to
watch the fight, but Sheriff Howie arrested the two principals
and there was no duel after all.

Just before Christmas, two men were shot in a saloon
for no particular reason, and the report on flour wagons was
that they couldn't get in until late in February. (That was an
optimistic prediction.) The next newspaper reported a prize
fight that went to 185 rounds and ended in a draw.

In February, the newspaper reported a fight in a dance
hall, but nobody was hurt. The February 18 issue was
printed on colored paper—the *Montana Post* had run out
of newsprint and could get no more.

In March, several hundred miles of telegraph wire across the plains had been put out of commission, either by weather or by Indians, so there was no outside news, but the *Post* had been able to get some paper from an army post in Wyoming. Stage coaches were getting through now and then, but no flour was coming in, and the price was going up. Mail took twenty days to come from Salt Lake City.

For a short period, merchants asked almost a dollar a pound for flour. Many single men voluntarily deprived themselves of bread, biscuits, or pancakes and lived almost entirely on meat and coffee so that families with children could buy the flour that was still available.

And in April, the flour famine resulted in dangerous riots. Public meetings were held, and committees of angry men called on the storekeepers to sell their hoarded flour at reasonable prices.

An armed mob formed, intending to take flour by force out of a warehouse where another armed mob was ready to defend it at gunpoint. The valiant Sheriff Howie and Colonel Sanders, who was both valiant and eloquent, talked them out of shooting one another.

The April 22 issue of the *Post* carried news of world-wide significance: General Robert E. Lee had surrendered to General Ulysses S. Grant on April 9, and the terrible Civil War was over. But this news got only nine lines of type in the *Post,* because the local news about flour was more important.

Almost five hundred silent, armed men had marched down Virginia's main street and had searched the town for hidden flour. They collected eighty-two sacks, gave receipts to the owners, stored the sacks in a public hall, and rationed the flour at a reasonable price, a few pounds to each family, as long as it lasted.

One day when Harriet Sanders was away from home, a

group of men entered her house and searched every nook and cranny, assuming that she had some flour hidden away. She had none. She was away from home because, like many other housewives, she was trudging from one store to another, trying to buy enough flour to make bread for her children.

The Montana Post for April 29 carried two news items of special importance: President Abraham Lincoln had been assassinated, and fourteen sacks of flour had come in from the mountains. Supplies of rice, beans, and hominy were almost gone.

The next week there was more big news: Lincoln's killer, John Wilkes Booth, had been shot, and sixty-four sacks of flour had come in on Monday. The price fell to sixty-five dollars. But traffic over the Continental Divide had stopped because the melting snow crust would not support mules or oxen. The animals simply sank out of sight. The flour that did come through had been unloaded three times and carried on men's shoulders for some distance. On Thursday, more than one hundred sacks were hauled into town.

The hungry winter was over—and people standing in the streets to watch the flour wagons roll by burst into tears of joy.

Something remarkable happened in Virginia City while the Sanders family lived there. Six camels came to town! Transportation was a serious problem in the West, and these swaying beasts of burden had been imported from the other side of the world in the hope that they could carry heavier loads and travel longer distances than other animals. These six were brought up from Arizona to be used as a pack train.

Such a commotion as they made! They scared the wits out of all the horses, and there were runaways in the streets whenever they appeared. (Some wit once defined a camel as a horse planned by a committee.)

In a desperate attempt at improving public relations, their owner offered free camel rides to the children of the town. The youngsters loved the camel master for that, but their fathers, mad and tired after quieting their snorting, rearing horses, said the camels had to go. Five of them were taken to Utah, but the other one strayed off and, late in June, 1865, was shot by a hunter who was startled to find that his big game was certainly not an elk.

While the Sanders family lived in Virginia City, Harriet decided to dispose of an old piece of carpet. A saloon keeper bought it and put it on the floor—not to make the place look homey, but because he knew it would make money for him.

There was little coin or paper currency in circulation; gold dust and nuggets were used to pay for everything. For substantial purchases, the gold was weighed on a scale, and every business establishment had a scale for that purpose. For small purchases, the buyer measured out his dust in pinches. Naturally some of the precious yellow dust accidentally sifted out from between thumb and forefinger—and the saloon keeper with the piece of carpet had his own private gold mine. Every now and then he washed the carpet and reclaimed the gold it had collected.

In the winter of 1866, Colonel Sanders took his wife and the two little boys back to Ohio for a visit. They traveled the luxurious way, by stagecoach—but "luxurious," in this case, didn't mean "comfortable." It meant expensive and relatively fast. If the road was not blocked with snow, a coach drawn by four or six good horses could cover 160 miles a day. The day included twenty-four hours of constant travel, and the journey jolted the passengers to the very marrow of their bones.

Meals at station stops were not very good; the Sanders

party missed several meals altogether through mismanagement by the stage company.

The Sanders family slept on the floor of the bouncing vehicle, wrapped in blankets and fur robes. They started on February 21, and on March 7 they were still traveling, with occasional stops for rest.

Harriet, who always looked on the bright side of things, noted in her journal: "Strange as it may seem, we are having a most comfortable journey. All are well, the boys happy, and we do not fail to enjoy it."

They reached St. Louis on March 16, and some friends gave the boys two oranges—a rare treat in those days.

The following spring, they went back to Montana. That was home now and for the rest of their lives, although the boys later went east to attend Phillips Exeter Academy and Harvard University and traveled in Europe.

On that return journey, in the spring of 1867, Colonel Sanders took the stage; it was fast, as transportation went, and he had business back home. Harriet and her mother and her two little boys, plus their young cousin, Eddie Upson, took a more leisurely route. They went by steamboat up the Missouri River to Fort Benton. What an expedition that was!

Mrs. Sanders and her party boarded the steamship *Abeona* at St. Joseph, Missouri, on April 24, the day before her thirty-third birthday. They didn't get to their river destination, Fort Benton, until late at night on the Fourth of July.

River travel was comfortable. It was also tediously slow. Steamboats kept getting stuck on sandbars; if the wind blew strongly, they couldn't move upriver for days at a time. Steamboat men were a wild lot; the boats sometimes raced—and never mind how that dangerous nonsense scared the lady passengers!

Missouri River steamboats didn't carry fuel, but stopped every now and then to let the men go ashore and cut wood. This took time, and the boilers of the *Abeona* kept breaking down. There were Indian scares, also—two boats ahead of the *Abeona* were attacked and one white man was killed.

That year, 1867, the Missouri River was a busy superhighway. There were times when thirty or forty steamboats were on the river between Fort Benton and the mouth of the Yellowstone River.

On June 24, the *Abeona* stopped for thirteen hours to "wood up." Next day she got stuck on a sandbar and the men had to throw every stick of wood overboard to lighten her. Harriet noted in her journal that everybody had "the blues." But they did reach Fort Benton at last, at eleven o'clock at night on July 4. Colonel Sanders, Harriet's husband, had given the Independence Day oration there that day. Even after seventy-two days of steamboat travel on the Missouri River, the family wasn't home yet.

At two o'clock the next morning they boarded a stage coach. They rode all day and the following night, reaching Helena at eight o'clock in the morning. They still weren't home, and they didn't get very much rest in Helena, because various people came to call, including two judges and a minister.

The party still had 120 miles to go by stagecoach to Virginia City. The trip took twenty-one hours. And after all that, less than a week after they reached home, Harriet Sanders went through the tribulations of moving into a new house!

Colonel and Mrs. Sanders had three more sons besides Jimmie and Willie. Louis, who became a lawyer, was born in 1870, and twin boys were born in 1872, but neither of those babies lived very long.

Helena became a more important town than Virginia City,

and in 1875 it became capital of the Territory. The same year the Sanders family built a fine house in Helena—but teen-agers Jimmie and Willie came very close to burning it down in an experiment prompted by laudable scientific curiosity.

Someone gave them a small balloon, which would ascend when heat was applied. They set fire to a sponge soaked in turpentine, and twice they got the balloon to rise as high as the house. Then the sponge dropped out and set fire to a neighbor's chicken coop.

Willie put out the fire and, still experimenting, the boys went up to the observatory of the grand house that wasn't quite finished and tried burning alcohol as fuel for the balloon. This time the balloon itself caught fire, and so did the floor. After putting out that fire, they quit experimenting.

Colonel Sanders was a busy, prosperous attorney with fruitful investments in various mining properties. He held many political offices, too. His wife led an active social life, making calls and entertaining guests, attending public lectures, and doing church work. She had a good life and was proud of her husband and her sons.

She had worries, as everyone does. For twenty-eight years, her husband had a cancerous condition on one eyelid. In 1901 he had an operation in Chicago and spent months in a hospital there. He died July 7, 1905.

Four years later, Harriet Sanders was visiting her youngest son, Louis, in Butte when she suffered an attack of gallstones. Major surgery was often fatal in those days, and she died on September 24, 1909, after an operation.

5

Some Married Badmen

❦

Electa Plummer and Maria Virginia Slade

ELECTA BRYAN, aged twenty, was visiting her relatives, the Vails, near Fort Benton on the Missouri River, late in 1862, when she met a handsome stranger. His name was Henry Plummer, and his companion was Jack Cleveland. The men had ridden in from the west, intending to take a boat down the Missouri, back to the United States.

Dozens of travelers came that way and found excuses to stay around for a while, because Electa was young, pretty, and single. Her sister, Mrs. Vail, was married to a man who ran a Government farm.

White women were scarce in that raw, rough territory, then part of Idaho. Electa had plenty of admirers. All of them rode in looking about the same—sweaty, unwashed, unshaven, wearing shapeless clothing the color of the dust.

Henry Plummer had something that most of the others lacked—good manners. He acted like a gentleman. He spoke quietly, using the language of an educated man. He was almost six feet tall, straight, slender, and handsome, with keen grey eyes. He was not yet thirty years old.

Plummer and Cleveland spent part of the winter near

the Government farm. They had a fight about Electa Bryan, but she probably never knew it. When they left, in the spring, Electa had promised to marry Henry Plummer, and he had changed his mind about going east. He would seek his fortune in the gold mines at Bannack instead.

Here are some of the things that the bride-to-be didn't know about her fiancé: A few years earlier he had opened a bakery in Nevada City, California, and had been elected city marshal. Henry Plummer was a dedicated woman chaser, and before his term of office ended he shot the husband of one of the women he chased. He spent a few months in prison for that murder but was released on the grounds that he was consumptive.

Plummer beat another man badly over the head with a pistol. He helped some other desperadoes hold up a Wells, Fargo treasure coach carrying gold, but his gun fell apart while he was trying to shoot the driver, who lashed his team and got away.

Then Plummer killed another man, went to jail, and escaped, probably by bribing the jailer. With another badman named Mayfield he rode north to Oregon Territory, after prudently sending word to several California newspapers that he had been hanged. That ought to discourage pursuit!

He drifted to the newly opened gold mines in Idaho and worked—if you can call it that—as a professional gambler, also as a "road agent," holding up travelers for their gold.

Those were just some of the things that his trusting future wife didn't know.

In Bannack he began to build a cabin that would be a snug home for his promised bride. In February, after an argument, he fired five shots at his old friend, Jack Cleveland, who died a few hours later. Not long after that, Plummer himself was seriously wounded in a shooting scrape. Both bones of his lower right arm were broken in two places, and the doctor could not extract the bullet because he couldn't find it. Plummer practiced shooting with his left hand, and a very good shot he was.

Henry Plummer was elected sheriff of the Bannack mining district in May, and in June he rode north to marry Electa Bryan. Then Sheriff Plummer and his bride moved into their cabin in Bannack.

Electa must have been proud to be the wife of a leading citizen who held public office and had plenty of money. (He said he got it from successful investments in mining properties.)

But she couldn't be proud of him for very long. In September she went east for a visit—and never came back. On January 4, her husband was hanged.

After the Vigilantes at Virginia City organized and started executing road agents, a little group of them rode over to Bannack and hanged the road agents' leader, Sheriff Plummer, with two of his deputies—on the same scaffold that Plummer had built for the hanging of a man he had arrested.

In Virginia City, even now, you can hear strange stories. An old man at Robber's Roost, twelve miles out of Virginia City, recently told the following:

"Up there on the balcony, the road agents used to sit and wait until the stage come along so they could rob it. The road used to be over that way, where they could see it, not along the back of the building, where it is now."

That much is true. On that rickety balcony, it's not hard to imagine those villains with their chairs tipped back, their booted feet up on the rail, and their hats tilted down over their eyes while they waited for a cloud of dust that heralded the stagecoach.

But the old man told something else that is not true:

"Mrs. Plummer used to hang a bed sheet on her clothesline over there in Virginia City to warn the boys that the stage was leaving."

This is legend—and pure nonsense. Electa Plummer never lived in Virginia City; she lived, during her brief, tragic marriage, in Bannack, seventy miles away. If any woman had hung out a sheet in Virginia City, it could not have been seen from Robbers' Roost. And Sheriff Plummer's bride left him and Montana behind her as soon as she found out what a villain he was.

After Henry Plummer was dead by hanging, his executioners found out what had become of that bullet that his doctor couldn't locate. It had lodged in his wrist, and the movement of the joint had kept it shiny and polished. Obviously, some ghoulish Vigilante, prompted by curiosity, performed a post-mortem operation.

Electa Plummer had been a widow for many years when she married a man named Maxwell. They had two sons. There is a story that she bore a child to Henry Plummer after he died at the end of a hangman's rope. It may be true.

*   *   *

Maria Virginia Slade, nicknamed Molly, was the wife of a violent man with a reputation as a killer. At least once, she saved his life. She was fiercely loyal to him until he died at the end of a hangman's rope. And—shh!—it is said that her ghost still rides by the house where they last lived.

Where Molly came from, and where and when she married Joseph Albert Slade, nobody remembers any more. What is remembered is that she was kind, she was faithful, she must have been lonely, and she made a wild ride to try to keep him from being hanged.

Joseph Slade was born in Illinois, the son of a United
States Congressman. In his early twenties he killed a man,
perhaps in self-defense, and disappeared into the wild West.
By the time Joe Slade was thirty, he was famous—or infa-
mous. He was never a bandit, but he took on a tough job,
and he was just the man for that job. He was employed by
the Overland Stage Line to clean out the horse and stock
thieves, holdup men, and other ruthless outlaws in a vast
area traversed by the company's stage coaches.

He did it. He was as ruthless as the outlaws. He shot some
men and hanged some others, and he himself was severely
wounded in one gunfight. Ben Holladay, owner of the Overland, warmly approved of the effectiveness of Joe Slade's
brutal methods, but the remaining outlaws naturally hated
him. They tricked him, captured him, and shut him up in
an isolated log cabin with every intention of killing him.

"Let me say good-bye to my wife," he implored. "You
know I can't get away. But let me see Molly just once before
you finish me off."

Very well; they'd grant the condemned man that much.
One of them saddled up and rode off to bring back Molly.
The outlaws decently stayed outside while she ran into the
cabin, crying, to say good-bye to Joe.

Immediately Joe appeared in the doorway with a gun in
each hand. Right behind him was his wife with another gun.
Keeping the outlaws covered, the Slades leaped to their saddles and galloped away. What Joe's captors hadn't foreseen
was that his wife was an ingenious woman who didn't give
up easily. She had smuggled those pistols into the cabin
under the full, flowing skirt of her riding habit.

A young traveler named Sam Clemens, who became world
famous as the writer Mark Twain, met Slade at one of the
Overland stage stations and wrote about the meeting in a

book, *Roughing It*. He described Slade as "the most gentle-
manly appearing, quiet and affable officer we had yet found
along the route in the Overland company's service"—but
this pleasant fellow had the awesome reputation of having
killed twenty-six men!

Slade insisted on pouring the last cup of coffee in the pot
for Sam Clemens, who said later that he almost died of fright
for fear this ferocious man would change his mind and decide, after the coffee was gone, that he wanted it himself.

Joe Slade was still working for the Overland when a saloon
keeper named Jules Savoie threatened to kill him. Joe casually ordered two of his men to "go and clean out old Savoie."
They did. Misinterpreting his orders, they killed Savoie and
his Indian wife in a fight and burned their cabin.

The Savoies had two small children. The little girl ran to
hide in the brush and froze to death there. The boy, Jemmie,
was adopted by the Slades, who were appalled at what had
happened. Nobody remembers how long he lived with them
or what became of him.

Another of Joe Slade's executions took place in the summer in 1860, not far from Independence Rock. A doctor
named Bartholomew was shot by two ruffians. He left a
widow and two small children. Mrs. Bartholomew fled for
protection to a storekeeper, and he wrote a letter to Slade,
who was superintendent of that division of the Overland.

Slade wrote back: "Sit in your store with a loaded shotgun
till I get there Friday. Have two lariats ready."

Slade and four other men arrived by stage coach on Friday
and used the lariats to hang the killers of Dr. Bartholomew.
Slade searched their pockets and found five hundred dollars,
which he gave to the widow. This was entirely illegal, of
course, but that's how Slade did things. Mrs. Slade gave Mrs.
Bartholomew half of her own dresses and made over some

clothes for the children. Slade took care of selling the Bartholomew ranch and livestock, to add to the widow's stake,
and gave her and her children a free pass to travel on the
stage. She went home to Omaha carrying a thousand dollars
in gold in a pillow case.

In the fall of 1863, the Slades moved on, settling down at
first in Virginia City, Montana. Joe brought with him a
reputation as a ruthless bully, but he met his match among
the gold miners and merchants there. They were tough, too.
He didn't kill anyone, he never robbed anyone, but more
and more often he drank too much and pushed people
around.

The territory had no effective government yet, so it had
no tax money to pay for building roads. Slade found a place
where a road was badly needed for wagon travel between
Virginia City and the Gallatin Valley, where there were
farmers on whose produce the miners depended for food.
Slade cleared out several miles for a passable wagon road
and charged each wagon a toll for using it. In a pleasant but
very isolated gully beside a stream he built a small stone
house.

There Mrs. Slade stayed with an Indian woman for company, and collected tolls from the mule skinners who used
the road. But Joe spent most of his time drinking down in
Virginia City. Sometimes he took a notion to ride his horse
right into a store, the way rowdies do in western movies.

During the winter of 1864 the Vigilantes caught and
hanged some two dozen of the vicious highwaymen known
as "road agents." The Vigilantes were angry, and they were
determined to make the gold gulches safe for peaceable
people.

Joe Slade tried their patience too far and too often. Early
in March, he went on such a rampage through town that

several merchants locked their stores to keep him out. Joe wasn't alone—he had plenty of roughneck friends who rode with him. On March 9, the sheriff tried to arrest him. Slade furiously tore up the warrant for arrest and then threatened the local judge with a revolver.

Over and over, he was warned by Vigilantes to quiet down and go home to the toll house. He kept putting off his departure—and he put it off too long. The Vigilantes took him in charge and decided to hang him.

One of his friends ran for a horse and galloped out to warn Molly. Terrified by the thought of what might happen to the man she loved in spite of his faults, she set out at once to try to save him. Molly Slade was a magnificent rider, and she had a famous black horse named Billy Bay.

Nobody now alive saw her ride down the hill into town, of course, but many people who still live there remember the way their grandparents described that frantic rescue effort. She came at breakneck speed, with her long black hair flying in the wind, and she screamed as she rode. She had a pistol in her hand.

But Molly Slade arrived a few minutes too late. Joe had been hanged from the crossbar of a corral in Daylight Gulch. His body had been cut down and taken to a room in the Virginia Hotel.

Molly railed at his executioners, many of whom had been his friends.

"Why didn't somebody shoot him instead of letting him hang?" she screamed. "No dog's death should have come to such a man!"

When she was able to pull herself together, some hours later, she resolved that the body of her beloved should not rest among his enemies. She would not permit it to be buried in Virginia City. She ordered a coffin made with a zinc lin-

ing and had it filled with alcohol as a preservative. She kept
the coffin, with Slade's body in it, until spring came. When
the snow in the mountains melted enough to permit travel,
she rode sadly out of town with the coffin in a wagon and
had the body buried in a cemetery in Salt Lake City.

With her, driving the team, went a friend of her late husband named Kiscadden. She married him, but they separated
later, and nobody knows the rest of the story of Molly Slade.

As the years passed, the toll house deteriorated. Part of the
roof fell in under the weight of winter snows. Wild horses
sometimes took refuge there in bitter weather. And a
legend grew: the place was haunted.

Travelers who passed that way said they could hear the
sound of galloping hoofs and the voice of grieving Molly
Slade crying through the wind as she made that frantic ride
over and over again, on her black horse with her long black
hair flying.

A lone traveler who took shelter in the empty house during
a blizzard was never seen alive again. His body was found the
following spring, after the snow melted.

The road doesn't go that way any more. Nobody goes near
the old toll house except, occasionally, a sheepherder guard-
ing his flock. But sheepherders never spend a night in the
ruined house where Joseph and Molly Slade used to live,
more than a hundred years ago. They don't want to hear her
crying through the wind.

6

Some Were Rebels

ᛡ

Dr. Bethenia Owens-Adair

BETHENIA OWENS was born in Missouri, February 7, 1840, and was actually one of the first of the pioneers. When she was three, the Owens family went west in an emigrant wagon and settled on the Clatsop plains in Oregon, at the mouth of the Columbia River.

They were among the very earliest of the westward movers along a route that became the famous Oregon Trail. The first caravan of settlers bound for Oregon and California had pulled out of Independence, Missouri, in the spring of 1841. Before that, only the Mountain Men—hardy, fearless fur trappers—and a handful of missionaries had crossed the vast, uncharted plains and the rugged Rocky Mountains.

Five white families were in Oregon before them. Two of the white men had Indian wives.

Bethenia's father, Thomas Owens, built a cabin, and his wife, Sarah, chinked it with ferns. (That is, she packed the spaces between the logs to keep out the cold.) Together they made a fireplace with chunks of sod chopped from the earth. Anything that had to be fastened together, such as the poles that were part of the roof, they tied with rawhide, because they had no nails.

Bethenia's mother was not a woman to complain, but when she was almost ninety she said that was the unhappiest year of her life—not because, as we might think, she had to work so hard, but because she had nothing to do!

There was no wool to spin, no yarn to knit, and nothing to sew. She was used to keeping busy, but she didn't even have rags to use for patching. Lack of a dish rag was her greatest annoyance. Then one day a neighbor gave her a little bundle of rags. Mrs. Owens said that never, before or after that, did she have a present that she appreciated so much.

There wasn't much cooking to do, either. Salmon and potatoes were the main foods available. For a long time the family could not even have bread because they could not get flour—there was no grist mill near. Mrs. Owens experimented. She parched wheat in a skillet over the fire, ground it in a small coffee mill, and mixed in mashed potatoes. After that, the family had bread on the table.

In some respects, the very early pioneers lived as the native Indians did, making do with what they could get. Even if you have money—and most of them did not—you can't buy things that aren't there.

Nobody in the Owens family had shoes or stockings during their first two years in Oregon. They wore moccasins, which Mrs. Owens made from deer skins, as the Indians did. Children usually went barefoot anyway, except in winter.

Country people in those days cultivated many skills. They had to be ingenious and self-reliant, even if they didn't go west. Mr. Owens knew how to make shoes. All that was lacking was the material. He tanned elk hide to make stout leather, and a neighbor made a last in the shape of a foot, over which the leather could be fitted.

Strong thread to sew leather was lacking, so Mrs. Owens provided that—but not right away. Linen thread is made from the fibers of flax. She had brought a handful of flax seed across the plains. She chopped the sod near her cabin into squares with an ax, removed the chunks to expose the soil beneath, and cultivated that soil with a small hoe, the only garden implement she had. Then she planted her treasured flax seed and waited for it to grow.

She was delighted with the abundance and quality of the crop. She had learned, in her girlhood, how to extract the fibers and spin them into thread, but she had no spinning wheel. A neighbor who had never even seen such a thing made one for her after she described what she wanted. With it she spun good, stout thread—and after all that, the Owens family could have shoes.

There was a ready market for the flax fiber, too—it was just what the Indians needed for making fishing nets. It was much superior to the twine they had been making from cedar bark. They traded great quantities of fine salmon for the flax fiber and didn't even ask to have it spun into thread.

Bethenia and her brothers and sisters had no problems about adjusting to doing without things that were obtainable only in more settled areas. The children didn't even know what they were missing. They grew up with the country, enjoying new comforts as these became available.

There were no tax-supported public schools with regular sessions for children in Oregon in those days. When Beth was twelve, a wandering teacher came to the community and ran a school for three months. That was the only formal education she had until several years later—but one of the remarkable things about her is that she became a doctor.

Bethenia was tiny, but very strong. Her favorite brother, Flem, was two years younger. When she was thirteen, he dared her to try to carry two hundred pounds of flour—and she managed it. Another day, in a wrestling match to decide which one of them had to feed the horses, she fell and broke off a front tooth. There were few dentists in that frontier country, and not until eighteen years later did she have that gap filled in—with a shining gold tooth of which she was very proud.

Beth was thirteen when she met a tall, handsome man named Legrand Hill—and she was fourteen when she married him, on May 4, 1854. She was so little that she could stand under his outstretched arm. (She attained her growth late. When she was twenty-five, she reached five feet, four inches.)

Legrand had two talents: hunting and loafing. He bought a farm (on credit), and brought in plenty of wild game for the table, but he had a strong antipathy toward work. Beth kept house in a rude log cabin only twelve by fourteen feet. It had neither floor nor chimney, because her shiftless husband never got around to building them. The couple had to depend on Beth's parents—who were certainly not prosperous —for everything except the meat Legrand brought in.

Beth cooked outside over an open fire even when it rained, having no place inside the cabin to let the smoke out. She used tin dishes, which she kept shining bright, and her other household equipment consisted of an iron cooking pot, an iron teakettle, an iron oven, a twenty-gallon iron pot for heating water, a churn, six milk pans, and a wash tub and scrubbing board. All these iron receptacles were, of course, very heavy to lift—and you can imagine how much shifting around had to be done in cooking a meal or doing a washing when there wasn't even a stove.

The milk pans were broad, flat containers in which the milk was kept (after obtaining it from the cow, which requires more skill than ordering it from a dairy) while the cream rose to the top. If you've never had any milk except the homogenized kind, in which the cream is thoroughly mixed in, you may not know how thick and luscious cream is on top of a pan of milk.

The cream was used to make butter—a food item that we take for granted now and buy casually at any grocery store. When a housewife judged that she had enough cream to make a batch of butter, she got out the churn and prepared for some physical labor. This vessel was usually made of heavy crockery, about as high as her knees. It had a wooden plunger, which she worked up and down for thirty to forty-five minutes until the butter "came"—that is, the cream formed lumps about the size of peas.

She wasn't through yet. She poured off the buttermilk and put it away to use for cooking or for the pigs or chickens to drink, and then washed the butter with water and worked salt into it with a wooden paddle.

Many people used to think that when the butter wouldn't "come" it was due to witchcraft. A more scientific explanation—though perhaps not *very* scientific—is that the cow was overheated from running before she was milked.

Young Bethenia was perfectly willing to work hard; everybody she knew worked hard—except her husband. The situation in their home became desperate after the baby was born, April 17, 1856. Little George was tiny, sickly, and cranky. Beth had typhoid fever that summer and was weak for a long time afterward.

Legrand was quick-tempered and brutal. He struck and choked his young wife just once too often, and after he whipped the baby unmercifully, Beth left her husband forever. Their neighbors considered this utterly disgraceful, but she refused to expose the baby to any more treatment of that kind.

At eighteen, with a two-year-old child to support and only three months of school, she felt that she would never again be well or happy. For a while she lived with her parents—there was plenty of work to do on their farm. Her health slowly improved, and she began to look toward the future.

Education might be the key to success, she thought—but she could barely read and write. When a school term opened half a mile from home, she asked her mother's permission to attend.

"The baby won't be any trouble," her mother said briskly. "The other children will look after him." And so, while Beth became an elementary pupil again, her younger brothers and sisters romped with little George.

Beth paid with hard work for everything she got. She arose very early every morning, helped milk the cows, and did all the housework she could before going to school. On Saturdays she washed and ironed and caught up with her homework. She advanced fast during that four-month term.

In the fall of 1859 she went through a humiliating ordeal —she applied for a divorce and custody of her child. The following spring the divorce was granted, and her maiden name was restored. Thereafter she was Mrs. Bethenia Owens. She liked her father's name so well that she kept it even after she married again, many years later.

For a year she earned her living by sewing and doing home nursing. Sometimes she took in washing, over the protests of her father.

In the fall of 1860 she went to Oysterville, Washington, to visit a girlhood friend. The friend begged her to stay, and Beth found the idea of going to school again very attractive. She was working toward the future, although she did not yet know what her goal was. She earned her board by helping with the housework, and for a little cash she did washings in the evening. But that couldn't go on indefinitely. She decided to teach school.

Her older sister, Diana, was married and lived in Astoria. Beth moved there, borrowed a horse, and rode around the community, soliciting pupils. She lined up sixteen children whose parents would pay her three dollars a month tuition for each child for three months. She got up at four o'clock every morning to do her share of the housework in her sister's home, and she did a great deal of studying at night, because three of her pupils were farther advanced than she was! Like many country-school teachers of that time, she kept ahead of them by cramming at home.

Wanting even more schooling for herself, she gave up teaching and moved into a boarding house in Astoria with her baby and her nephew, Frank. She was utterly humiliated when, in the school preparatory examinations, she did so badly in mental arithmetic that she was placed with the primary children for that subject. But the principal helped her study, and in a few weeks she advanced to the highest class.

The following year she set up housekeeping in three small rooms, living frugally and saving her money while continuing in school. She sewed, crocheted, did big washings, picked up firewood along the beach, and was able to earn about five dollars a week with all this work. She learned to iron with a book open in front of her, because her study time was limited.

Things were looking up for Bethenia Owens! She was both contented and happy, and she was independent. She valued her independence so much that when a middle-aged river bar pilot offered to send her to school anywhere in the

United States as long as she cared to attend, she refused because she could not endure the thought of being under obligation to anyone. Sometimes in later years she bitterly regretted that decision.

Her luck held. So did her health and her ambition. She got a job teaching school for three months at twenty-five dollars a month. She paid for her board by cleaning nine rooms of a private boarding house. In addition, she took two advanced courses in school and even found time to attend a reading and singing class one night a week.

She moved from one teaching job to another—and then changed her career completely. She set up a millinery and dressmaking business in Roseburg and prospered greatly. She even went to San Francisco for a while to learn advanced millinery skills in order to compete with a woman who set up a shop in competition with hers.

But she was not satisfied. She considered a new career. She liked caring for sick people, and she decided to become a doctor.

When her son George was fourteen, she entered him in the University of California at Berkeley. It was customary then for young people to go from elementary school directly into college if they could pass the examinations. Our present secondary-school system was not established until 1885.

Then Bethenia Owens turned her highly successful business over to a younger sister and announced that she was going to Philadelphia to attend medical school.

This news horrified her relatives and friends. A woman doctor? What an outrageous idea! She was ruining her life, they said, and disgracing her family. Even her son felt that she was doing him a terrible wrong. She went anyway, but when her stagecoach started out, she was crying.

In Philadelphia she attended the Eclectic School of Medicine and in addition employed a private tutor and attended lectures and clinics in a hospital. Eclectic doctors practiced on the theory that each disease had a specific remedy. Most of these remedies were made from herbs.

Beth earned her degree and went home to close up her millinery business. She could not practice as a fully qualified physician because of her limited training, but she could practice medicine to some extent.

A few days after her return to Roseburg, an old man died, and six physicians decided to hold an autopsy on his body. One of them, Dr. Palmer, considered Bethenia Owens impudent for presuming to take up a profession that was open only to men, and with the idea of embarrassing her, he recommended that she be invited to take part in the autopsy. That would show her up!

To the horror of the six doctors, she came.

Dr. Palmer was furious. "I object to a woman's being present at a male autopsy," he stormed, "and if she is allowed to remain, I shall leave!"

"I came here by written invitation," Dr. Beth replied stoutly. "You can vote on whether I may stay, but I'd like to know what's the difference between a woman being present at a male autopsy and a man being present at a female autopsy!"

Five of the doctors agreed that she might remain, and Dr. Palmer walked out in a huff. In a real effort to embarrass the new woman doctor, the others handed her the instruments and let her do the dissection.

She was the talk of the town. Everyone was scandalized. Later she realized that feeling ran so high that she might have been tarred and feathered, but the fact that two of her brothers lived in the town saved her. Flem and Josiah disapproved of her actions as much as anyone, but they defended her because she was their sister. Everyone knew they would shoot at the drop of a hat, so nobody offered any violence.

She closed up her business and, taking her sister along, moved to Portland, knowing that her family was glad to have her out of Roseburg. She opened an office with special baths for the treatment of rheumatism. Patients began to come to her, and she began to earn a very good income.

Her son George, now nineteen, entered the medical department of Willamette University and two years later could write M.D. after his name, according to the requirements of the times.

When a woman patient died of double pneumonia, leaving three puny little girls, Dr. Beth adopted the oldest and smallest of them, Mattie, who was fourteen.

Bethenia Owens became prosperous, but she wasn't satisfied. She had plans for the future. First she took care of her responsibilities. She sent a sister to college and set up her son with a drug store. She sold property she owned and found that she had $8,000.

When she announced that she was going to medical school again, her relatives protested as they had the first time—but now they argued, "But you'll soon be rich if you simply go along as you are now! Don't gamble everything you've earned."

On September 1, 1878—she was thirty-eight years old—she left Portland again for the East. She was determined to attend Jefferson College in Philadelphia, but she was refused admittance. No woman had ever gone there. The University of Michigan, at Ann Arbor, had an excellent medical school, however, and she was accepted there.

For nine months she averaged sixteen hours a day attending lectures, working in clinics and laboratories, and studying. During the summer she studied ten hours a day. On

Sunday, the day of rest, she did not study at all; she went to church twice instead.

After two years—in June, 1880—she received a real medical degree. She had missed just one class, because she was so absorbed in her studies that she hadn't heard the bell. This lapse almost broke her heart.

There was more that she wanted to learn. For six months she lived in Chicago, working in hospitals and clinics. Her son, Dr. George Hill, joined her there and took postgraduate work.

Then Beth and her son and two women physicians sailed for Europe, where they traveled extensively.

Dr. Beth returned to Portland with only two hundred dollars left of the eight thousand she had started with, but the expenditure had been well worth while. She was no longer a "bath doctor," treating rheumatism.

She performed many surgical operations, and her medical practice was very lucrative. Her adopted daughter, Mattie, came to live with her. Later Beth wrote, "Had I had a hundred children, I am sure none could have been more faithful or loved me better." Mattie, too, graduated in medicine but did not practice. She died very suddenly while she was still quite young.

Dr. Beth had always said she would not marry again because she was married to her profession. But in 1884, she met a childhood friend, Colonel John Adair, and on July 24 of that year they were married. She added his last name to hers and was Dr. Owens-Adair thereafter. She continued with her medical practice, which gave her an annual income of seven thousand dollars—a very large sum in those days. She worked hard to earn it, too, with office calls at only two dollars each.

Colonel Adair had an optimistic plan to reclaim some tidelands property that he hoped would make a fortune. His wife invested in the plan, in spite of the advice of friends that it would lose money. It did.

When Dr. Beth was forty-seven, she gave birth to a daughter—thirty-one years after her son was born! The baby lived only three days. The mother was so grief-stricken that she could not endure to continue her practice in Portland when her husband was working on his reclamation project in Astoria. She moved there, to be near him, and practiced medicine successfully for two years. Then she became so sick from a fever that she fully expected to die. While she was slowly recovering, Colonel Adair told her, "Your health absolutely demands a change. On the farm, you'll get back your strength. Railroad trains will be running across our land in a couple of years, and we'll be rich. You'll never have to work again."

She agreed to go to their farm, near Seaside, Oregon, but later she realized that the move was one of the greatest mistakes in her life. She regained her health, but the bonanza the Colonel promised never arrived, and she continued her medical practice under terrible conditions. The farm was isolated, but she never refused to go out on a call, day or night, no matter how foul the weather was. She waded through flooded swamps, rode in open boats, fought through dense undergrowth in forests.

Sometimes her husband had to be away on business. Then she ran the farm, spending hours in the saddle looking after the livestock. She became partially crippled with rheumatism, and Colonel Adair insisted that she try the climate of North Yakima, Washington, for a while. She visited her son there, and the dry climate did wonders for her health.

"Why don't you set up a practice here?" Dr. George urged. "Let the farm go. You should never have gone there anyway. The damp climate will cripple you for life."

Dr. Beth agreed to make the move. Colonel Adair warned, "It's a terrible thing to make a change like that at our age and give up our home."

"Our home is covered with mortgages," she replied. "We owe twenty-four thousand dollars, and we're going farther into debt because of the high interest charges. We'd better give it all up and start over."

She practiced surgery and medicine in North Yakima. The summer of 1899, when she was fifty-nine years old, she spent at the Chicago Clinical School and earned a post-graduate degree. She retired from practice in 1905.

Bethenia Owens-Adair was a woman of firm opinions. When she had something to say, she said it, often in letters to newspapers. For instance, she thought women should be allowed to vote. A sweet old lady, utterly shocked at this outlandish idea, raised her hands in horror and exclaimed, with tears in her eyes, "I know nothing about this woman's movement, but I am bitterly opposed to it." There's open-mindedness for you!

Dr. Beth wrote this for publication in a newspaper:

> All that we ask, all that we entreat, is that our cause shall be investigated, analyzed, sifted, and if it be not the true metal, or solid principle, let it burn, like dross. The right of suffrage is an inalienable right, withheld wrongfully from woman by her brother man. No human being who will reasonably and conscientiously investigate this principle will fail to become a convert to it.

When, in 1886, the Women's Christian Temperance Union of Multnomah County, in Oregon, decided to work at the polls, trying to persuade the men to vote for their candidates, Dr. Beth helped with the planning. The ladies set up a stand half a block from each polling place and passed out temperance literature.

A man who signed himself "Orsini" wrote pleadingly in a newspaper that it wasn't the duty of true ladies to work at the polls, "to be jeered, insulted, scorned and scoffed at, perhaps cursed."

The reasons he gave seem funny to us now. He argued, "Ladies, your good, kind husbands would not care to see you at the polls, amid a crowd of shouting, noisy men, mingling among such besotted wretches, drunkards staggering, swearing, in such conditions as you would not care to see. . . . Your son would not have you see the wretched sights so common in such places, and horrifying to ladies."

The ladies went anyway. How could any red-blooded woman refuse, after such a challenge? Election day is pretty peaceful since women gained the right to vote.

Dr. Beth had another idea that some people thought was wild-eyed: she favored physical exercise for women. For pale, nervous patients she prescribed daily horseback rides in addition to medicine. When she was in her fifties, riding astride became fashionable, or at least acceptable, for women. Dr. Beth put her sidesaddle away, rode "in the new style," and advised her patients to do the same.

Nowadays we seldom see a woman riding sidesaddle except occasionally at a horse show. This used to be the only proper way for women to ride, however. A sidesaddle has a stirrup for the left foot, and the rider's right knee rests over a big leather hook at the front. Both feet are thus on the same side of the horse. The body is somewhat twisted, so for long rides the position is tiring. Just the same, that's how women rode, some of them for thousands of miles, with their limbs (not legs—ladies didn't admit to having legs) concealed under voluminous riding skirts.

During most of her long life, Dr. Beth shocked people with her modern notions. A woman couldn't become a doctor—

but she did. Women shouldn't vote—but we do. She spoke out in favor of change, and other people listened.

She thought skating was a fine thing, and welcomed the establishment of a skating rink in Portland, but conservative citizens attacked it as immoral. (This idea was not peculiar to Portland, either.) Dr. Beth took pen in hand and informed them, through the local newspaper, that she had visited the rink several times and was pleased to report that she had seen no improper behavior.

Customs have changed so much that we can't understand what could have been thought immoral about a public skating rink. What kind of improper behavior, for goodness' sake, is possible on skates?

7

Some Followed Adventure

❦

Isabella Bird and Elizabeth Custer

ONE OF THE MOST REMARKABLE TOURISTS who ever traveled in the American West just to see what it was like was Isabella Bird, a well-to-do, cultivated Englishwoman who journeyed through the Rocky Mountains in the fall and winter of 1873. She went all alone.

Miss Bird simply liked to travel, no matter how great the difficulties, and travel she did. She had no companion for protection—in a time when it wasn't customary for a woman to travel alone anywhere, and certainly not in an area that was still the Wild West—but she went anyway. "Intrepid" is the word for Isabella.

Unlike the other women in this book, Miss Bird actually did not go west. She went east, on her way home to England after a tour of the Sandwich Islands, now the state of Hawaii. She was forty-two, and she was recuperating from a severe illness. The hardships of the journey she undertook with the idea of improving her health would make most healthy people think twice, but apparently she thrived, for she lived another thirty-one years.

Miss Bird was a superlative reporter. She wrote long letters to her sister, Henrietta, which were later published as a book entitled *A Lady's Life in the Rocky Mountains*. Her book opens with these words, written at Lake Tahoe, on the border between California and Nevada:

"I have found a dream of beauty at which one might look all one's life and sigh." She loved the scenery of the western United States—and she was fascinated by the people, but she liked them only in small doses.

California, she wrote, was a land of milk and honey, but she found Sacramento "repulsive." She didn't think much of the Digger Indians, but neither did anyone else. They were, she wrote, very short people, hideous, filthy, and swarming with vermin, and she had heard that they lived almost entirely on grasshoppers.

Miss Bird could put up with almost any accommodations. She had to. The first qualification for a tourist in those days was adaptability. At Truckee, California, the hotel had so many tenants that they slept in eight-hour shifts. Miss Bird had a room with men's coats hanging on hooks, muddy boots scattered around, and a rifle in one corner. But she was so tired that she slept well—except for being awakened once by a series of pistol shots.

Next morning she put on her "Hawaiian riding dress," as she called it, and set forth to rent a horse. This costume, in a time when women invariably wore skirts, was both decent and practical, but it must have been a sight to behold. She described it as "a half-fitting jacket, a skirt reaching to the ankles, and full Turkish trousers gathered into frills over the boots." It was made of flannel.

There was the problem of a saddle. For the kind of rough trails her horse would take, a sidesaddle would be exhausting and unsafe, but a man told her that women thereabouts never rode astride. She almost gave up the idea of going for a ride, so powerful are the bonds of propriety, but the same man advised, "Ride your own fashion. Here at Truckee, if anywhere in the world, people can do as they like." Miss Bird loved Truckee from then on. One of the great attractions of the frontier West was that people *could* do as they liked.

While she was riding alone through the woods, her horse was panicked by a bear. The horse went one way, the bear went the other, and Miss Bird went over the side to land in the dust. After following the horse for a mile, she picked up the saddle blanket and then her bag of clothing, but she couldn't catch the horse. Some men driving an ox team succeeded, however, and she got back into the saddle and showed the horse who was boss. A little later she came upon a mother bear with two cubs, but the horse was still convinced that he should behave as his rider insisted.

Miss Bird met a few men on that ride, and she remarked that they might have been excused for speaking boldly to a lady alone, but "womanly dignity and manly respect for women are the salt of society in this wild West."

That evening she heard some fearsome stories. Two nights before, a man had ridden through the street with a chopped-up human body in a sack behind his saddle. Miss Bird was assured, however, that the ugliest of ruffians wouldn't touch her, because westerners admired nothing so much as courage in a woman.

Her next stop was Cheyenne, Wyoming. To get there, she traveled in a luxurious train, sleeping in a good bed with linen sheets and clean blankets. The train was quiet and did not jolt—it never ran at more than eighteen miles an hour.

She found Cheyenne "detestable." She was informed that 120 ruffians had been lynched there in two weeks. (Possibly the people of Cheyenne were enjoying this chance to tell tall

tales to the English lady.) Even more shocking was her con-
clusion that greed had taken the place of common humanity
in the West. Miss Bird did her best to help a sick and needy
family whom everyone else was ignoring.

Miss Bird was observant and interested in everything. She
wrote that many of the people she met were grim and silent.
In a boarding house in Greeley, Colorado—where she helped
the landlady get supper because the hired girl had quit—
twenty men in working clothes came in, ate, and went out
again without ever saying a word. Maybe they weren't so
untalkative by nature, though. What the English tourist
probably didn't know was that in some places, where many
men had to be fed in a hurry, there was a definite rule against
conversation because it slowed down eating.

Still observing, Miss Bird journeyed by wagon to Fort Col-
lins, where she was interested to see men galloping in from
the prairie to vote because it was election day. There was
shameless conversation about the price of votes and corruption in government. As far as Miss Bird could tell, *all* the
candidates were corrupt. Miss Bird simply wasn't accustomed to the mud-slinging that is usually a feature of an
election campaign in the United States. Where she came
from, elections were less exciting.

She saw something that none of us will ever see: a trail
herd of five thousand head of cattle moving slowly from
Texas to Iowa (they had already been traveling for several
weeks) with twenty cowboys shoving them along. The cowboys were heavily armed to ward off attacks by Indians who,
she wrote, were maddened by the useless, reckless slaughter
of the buffalo that were their staff of life.

The climate of the Colorado Rockies was believed to be
a cure-all for many diseases. Miss Bird met dozens of desperately sick people in the Rockies who were certainly not go-

ing to get any better, but she also met many who had recovered blooming health. Thousands of people suffering from tuberculosis, asthma, stomach trouble, or nervous diseases took the "camping cure," roughing it out of doors. In spite of the discomforts, an astonishing number of them did recover.

The intrepid Isabella could make no advance reservations and had no choice of luxurious hotels or motels. She stayed wherever someone was willing to take her in as a boarder, and she adjusted to existing circumstances. On the way to Estes Park, her destination, Miss Bird stopped at the rundown Chalmers farm, where Mrs. Chalmers reluctantly accepted her as a boarder if she would "make herself agreeable." Miss Bird looked over the accommodations offered— a one-room cabin with one wall partially broken down and holes in the roof—then sent back the buggy in which she had come and moved in.

The family made no effort to be agreeable. They were ignorant and uncouth. A young girl sat and stared at her but would not talk. Three other children pretended she wasn't there. Their manners were deplorable, and they were amazed every time Miss Bird said "Thank you."

When, trying to make herself agreeable, she offered to wash dishes, Mrs. Chalmers sneered, "Those hands of yours never done nothing, I guess."

But Isabella came up in their estimation when she made a lamp from a wisp of rag in a tin of fat. They had no light except from the fire. (They must have been unimaginative as well as bad-mannered. Lamps made from a rag for a wick, in a dish of fat or oil, were in common use five thousand years ago!)

Clothing was bulky in those days, so Miss Bird carried very little of it. Each day she washed one or two items of apparel (a calf chewed up some of her underwear that had been spread out to dry) and did some necessary mending.

She passed the time by knitting, which fascinated the Chalmers family, so she started a class with three pupils. She was knitting a quilt—we would call it an afghan—for her sister. If it seems strange to carry all that along in limited baggage, consider how strange it was that these frontier women did not even know how to knit.

Mr. Chalmers was a sour fellow who asked Miss Bird many questions about her travels, but he was so narrow minded that when she spoke favorably about any of the places where she had been, he felt that she was insulting Colorado. However, he thought more of her when she proved that she needed no help in saddling a horse.

Everything the Chalmers family did was, in Miss Bird's opinion, quite wrong. Everything was falling apart, nobody planned in advance, and she wrote, "It is hardly surprising that nine years of persevering shiftlessness should have resulted in nothing but the ability to procure the bare necessities of life."

If you are accustomed to thinking of all western pioneer families as admirable, industrious people of strong character, it is well to realize that there were many like the Chalmers family.

Mr. and Mrs. Chalmers unwillingly accompanied Miss Bird on a trip to beautiful Estes Park, about which she had heard a great deal. As usual, everything they did went wrong. The horses were in poor condition. Bullheaded Mr. Chalmers got the party lost. Next morning the horses were gone, because he had stubbornly refused to picket them. There was no water to drink; the canteen had no cork, and the water had spilled out when a pack mule fell the day before. They did find the horses, and they finally drank water,

thick as pea soup, from a mud hole, but the incompetent Mr,
Chalmers never did lead the way to Estes Park.

Isabella felt better when she visited some neighbors who
had built a snug little log house and made some effort to deco-
rate it with white muslin curtains and even some books on a
shelf. But these delightful people, Dr. and Mrs. Hughes,
were a fine example, Miss Bird decided, of those who should
not move to frontier Colorado. Dr. Hughes had not known
how to saddle or harness a horse or milk a cow. His wife
couldn't cook. They were charming, educated, cultured people, but they simply did not belong on a raw little farm in
the Rocky Mountains.

While Isabella visited the Hughes family, she more than
earned her keep. She plotted that their Swiss hired girl
should take two of the children to a neighbor's house so that
Dr. and Mrs. Hughes could have an afternoon of rest. Then
she did a washing, very pleased with the convenience of a
wringer that screwed on the edge of a tub. She baked bread,
scoured the churn and milk pails, and was washing some pans
when a teamster came along and asked where he could ford
the river. He looked pityingly at Miss Bird and asked, "Be
you the new hired girl? Bless me, you're awful small!"

Another day, she helped harvest three hundred pounds
of tomatoes and two tons of squash and pumpkin for winter
cattle feed. In addition, she pulled the ears off nearly a quarter of an acre of corn.

She had almost given up hope of seeing Estes Park, which
she had been told contained the most beautiful scenery in
Colorado, when she heard about two young men who were
going to make the trip. She rented a horse—although she was
still lame and bruised from a fall several days before—and set
out with them. On this journey they came to a hut, so rude
and dilapidated that it looked more like an animal's den.

The lone occupant was a desperado who made a great impression on the lady tourist. She never quite admitted it in her letters to her sister, but it's plain when you read between the lines that Miss Bird fell in love with Mountain Jim Nugent.

He wore ragged clothes that would have fallen off him except that he had a scarf knotted around his waist. There was a knife in the scarf, and a big revolver stuck out of his pocket. He was about forty-five. One side of his face was strikingly handsome. The other side had been clawed by a grizzly bear, and one eye was missing. He wore a mustache and the kind of beard called an imperial, and his golden, uncared-for hair hung in long curls.

This remarkable man, both attractive and repulsive, spoke like an educated gentleman and, like Miss Bird, he was from England. He made his living by trapping. She wrote of him, "He is a man for whom there is now no room, for the time for blows and blood in this part of Colorado is past." He was chivalrous, but he had an evil temper, and everyone was afraid of him.

But this man, Mountain Jim, became the guide for Miss Bird and her two young companions. He was, she commented, "as awful-looking a ruffian as one could see." He was a man of culture and a child of nature. When he learned that Miss Bird was unarmed, he was shocked and insisted that she carry a revolver thereafter.

She did climb Longs Peak, but the experience was embarrassing. When she was exhausted from exertion and paralyzed by fear, Mountain Jim dragged her up, like a bale of merchandise, by sheer muscle power. One part of the climb, about five hundred feet, took them an hour. The two young men were exhausted, too, and one of them was bleeding from the lungs.

Late in September, Miss Bird settled down to spend some

weeks in Estes Park at the ranch of two families named Evans and Edwards, who ran an establishment that would now be called a dude ranch. They had one big log cabin and two smaller ones and took in paying guests. For eight dollars a week, Isabella had a very rude cabin to herself, a horse, and her board. Every meal, including breakfast, featured beef, potatoes and new bread.

Her cabin door had no lock, but it wouldn't shut anyway. On her first night there, after her candle had burned out, she was awakened by what she thought was some large animal pushing under the floor. There was nothing she could do to protect herself, and in the morning she was surprised to see that her hair hadn't turned white as she expected. The noisy animal, she was told, had been a skunk sharpening its claws.

On October 9, the mail came—by wagon, after long delay—and with it came bad news. There was financial panic in the eastern United States. It had spread to the West, and all the banks in Denver had suspended business. They refused to cash checks on customers' accounts. Nobody could draw out even a dollar. Miss Bird wrote to her sister:

"Business is suspended, and everybody, however rich, is for the time being poor. The Indians have taken to the 'war path' and are burning ranches and killing cattle. There is a regular 'scare' among the settlers, and wagon loads of fugitives are arriving in Colorado Springs. The Indians say, 'The white man has killed the buffalo and left them to rot on the plains. We will be revenged.' "

Miss Bird had sent a hundred-dollar note with Evans when he went for the mail because she needed smaller bills to pay for her board. She was shocked when he came back without any money for her at all—he had been obliged to spend it for supplies, since he couldn't get money from a bank. Later he repaid her, but she was worried for some time. She was planning a trip of several hundred miles.

But she did not leave at once, because she was needed to help drive some wild cattle. Along with her other skills, the handy Miss Bird developed into a pretty useful cowboy! She was adaptable and, although critical, she didn't complain. She realized that she didn't really need anything more than her cabin offered. Cleaning it up took about five minutes, and it needed no lock because there was nothing in it worth stealing.

Some halcyon days passed as she went on roughing it and riding almost daily with the fascinating Mountain Jim. The children in the household adored him. When he came, they climbed on his broad shoulders and played with his curls.

"Ruffian as he looks," she wrote, "the first word he speaks —to a lady, at least—places him on a level with educated gentlemen, and his conversation is brilliant and full of the light and fitfulness of genius. Yet, on the whole, he is a most painful spectacle. His magnificent head shows so plainly the better possibilities which might have been his. His life, in spite of a certain dazzle which belongs to it, is a ruined and wasted one, and one asks what of good can the future have in store for one who has for so long chosen evil?"

There was not, in fact, very much future for Mountain Jim. He had less than a year to live.

On October 18, she wrote that the ranch had been snowbound for three days. She went to bed in her cabin under six blankets and awoke to find the cabin being shifted by the wind and the sheet frozen to her lips. The bed was covered with snow. The water bucket was solid ice. In the morning, some of the men came from the main cabin to dig her out and brought a can of hot water—which froze before she could use it.

All the guests crowded into the main room of the bigger cabin, wrapped in coats, with a huge fire going in the fireplace, and one of the hunters devoted himself to keeping Miss Bird's ink thawed out so that she could write. After the storm, she rode—all alone—to Denver, which she noted with approval was not so wild a town as she had heard.

"A shooting affray in the street is as rare as in Liverpool," she commented, "and one no longer sees men dangling on the lamp posts when one looks out in the morning!"

The tireless Miss Bird went on traveling, riding a mare called Birdie, which she learned to love. Birdie, intelligent, good-tempered, tireless, and sure-footed, was the queen of ponies.

Isabella never knew what accommodations she would find for the night, but she always had a roof over her head. Once, with her freet frozen (the temperature was nine degrees below zero), she had to ride past a cabin becuase it was crowded with seventeen men sleeping on the floor. At the next house, there were two women who ministered to her tortured feet.

She rode gaily on. Having no baggage except one small pack, and having a horse for transportation, she could go anywhere she dared. She really preferred staying in private homes rather than hotels, because she gained insight into the way the settlers lived. Once she enjoyed real luxury—after a supper that included venison and fried rabbit, she went to bed in a room with a carpet, a thick feather bed, sheets, ruffled pillow slips, and warm white blankets—and slept for eleven hours.

Miss Bird commented on corruption in government at every level. She was shocked because sharp practices seemed to excite the admiration of the American people. She observed the government's treatment of Indians and wrote, "The Indian Agency has been a sink of fraud and corruption; it is said that barely thirty per cent of the allowance ever reaches those for whom it is voted; and the complaints of shoddy blankets, damaged flour, and worthless firearms are universal. . . . An attempt has recently been made to cleanse the Augean stable of the Indian Department, but it has met with signal failure, the usual result in America of every effort to purify the official atmosphere."

The dauntless Isabella traveled five hundred miles on horseback, all alone in winter weather—for snow and cold come early in the high Rockies—never sure where she would find her next meal and shelter for the night. As long as her money lasted, she paid for accommodations. But the panic continued, and she could not cash what she called her "circular notes"—perhaps a forerunner of the travelers' checks that we use now when we're away from home. She could not start back to England.

In November, still traveling, Miss Bird noted that after she had paid her bill in Longmount, Colorado, she would have exactly twenty-six cents left. She went back to Estes Park because she could live at the Evans-Edwards ranch without money. On the way, guess who came riding along—the desperado Mountain Jim, of course! (She always wrote of him as "Mr. Nugent" and called him that, too. Such formality is no doubt wise in dealing with so dangerous a fellow.)

She did not in the least regret returning to the ranch. If anyone ever loved the Colorado Rockies, it was Isabella Bird. She called Estes Park "my grand, solitary, uplifted, sublime, remote, beast-haunted lair." But she had not intended to stay there indefinitely.

To her dismay, the Edwards and Evans families had moved away for the winter (although Evans himself was coming

back), and the food supply at the cabin was very low. Two
hunters, named Kavan and Buchan, were "batching" there.
They agreed that it would be a good idea for Miss Bird to
do some of the cooking and housework, because that would
give them more time to hunt. They made their living by selling wild meat in town.

These arrangements lasted for almost a month. Miss Bird
and the two men divided the work among them. Kavan made
excellent bread. The men cared for the milch cows and cut
wood for the roaring fire. Miss Bird cooked and constantly
swept mud and ashes off the floor—with a buffalo's tail, because the broom was gone. She made puddings and cakes as
long as the scant supply of materials held out, but there were
no vegetables except potatoes, and there was very little meat
except pickled pork, which she detested. Part of a beef carcass, stored in a shed, had spoiled.

Sometimes the men chopped a hole in the ice and brought
in mountain trout. Finally they sacrificed an elk carcass that
they had intended to sell. They needed the meat more than
they needed the money it would bring in the nearest town.
Even so, supplies ran out, and the three sojourners cut their
meals down to two a day.

Mountain Jim came to call now and then. He told the dark
tale of his misspent life to the sympathetic Miss Bird. He was
truly a man with two faces—one side superbly handsome,
the other ruined and scarred. Once, riding beside her, he
cried, "Now you see a man who has made a devil of himself!
Lost! Lost! Lost!" Her soul dissolved in pity, she said in a
letter to her sister.

Food was becoming very scarce. Isabella cherished a small
amount of very old buttermilk, which she used as leavening
for rolls, and Mr. Kavan made yeast for his bread from flour
and water set near the stove to sour.

SOME FOLLOWED ADVENTURE   113

Food wasn't the only thing that was almost gone. Miss Bird's shoes were worn out. She had left now only one change of underwear—and one day when that was hanging on the clothesline to bleach, a sudden furious wind ripped it into narrow strips. She mended her woolen stockings until they were nothing but darns, and whenever her flannel riding dress had to be mended, she sat by the fire wearing a black silk gown with a train!

Even with a huge fire blazing, the cabin temperature sometimes couldn't be raised above twenty degrees—twelve degrees below freezing.

The English lady co-operated in the celebration of that truly American holiday, Thanksgiving. She made pudding, for which she had saved eggs (one of the hens sometimes laid) and cream (one cow still gave a little milk) for several days. Dried cherries took the place of currants. A bowl of custard served as pudding sauce. Dinner included venison steak and potatoes, but tea had to be made from tea leaves that had already been used. Mountain Jim was invited to the feast, but he was in a savage mood and refused. The other men were afraid of him, anyway.

Isabella doubted whether anyone in America enjoyed Thanksgiving more than she and her two companions did, but she was English to the marrow. When the three of them sat by the fire singing, to pass the time, she was offended because Kavan and Buchan sang "My country, 'tis of thee" to the tune of *her* country's national anthem, "God save our gracious Queen."

Early in December, she left Estes Park to visit some friends, get her mail, and try to find Evans, who still had her hundred-dollar bill. A few miles along on her journey, she was terrified by the sight of a human figure, white with snow, and the flash of a pistol close to her ear. Mountain Jim had come through the storm to pay his respects in his own dramatic way!

She found Evans, they straightened out their finances, and she went on—with the temperature at seventeen degrees below zero.

After she returned to the cabin, a stranger came to call—"strikingly handsome, well dressed, and barely forty, with sixteen shining gold curls falling down his collar." She had to look again to discover that this was the desperado, Mountain Jim, all slicked up for once. She observed that Evans was never comfortable when Jim Nugent was around. She suspected that they hated each other.

Her next letter was written from Cheyenne on December 12. She had left her beloved Estes Park for the last time. Evans had ridden with her to Mountain Jim's den, where the two men shook hands in friendly fashion. (The following September, Evans fired the rifle bullet that killed Jim.)

Mountain Jim rode with her the rest of the way. At the places where they stayed, the women were very favorably impressed by the desperado. These were women who were in the habit of threatening their youngsters by warning, "If you don't behave, Mountain Jim will get you!" The same children, when actually confronted by this ogre, climbed all over him.

Miss Bird wrote, "As I looked at him, I felt a pity such as I never before felt for a human being." He felt it was too late for him to change, to reform. He had committed too many crimes. He was wanted by the law.

Miss Bird took the wagon stage to Greeley, and the last time she saw Mountain Jim he was riding away, with his golden hair yellow in the sunshine. A few hours later, as she rode across the plains, the Rocky Mountains went down below the prairie sea.

She traveled in other lands after that. She worked to found a college for medical missionaries. She spent the year 1878 in Japan and the Malay Peninsula. In 1889, she traveled in India and Tibet and tried to set up a hospital at Nazareth, but the Turkish government prevented this. She founded five other hospitals in cities in Asia. In her middle sixties, she traveled for eight thousand miles in China.

Isabella Bird wrote many books about her travels. She took pictures, too, in the days when a photographer had to cope with a great deal of clumsy equipment. In 1892 she was elected a Fellow of the Royal Geographical Society, the first woman to achieve that distinction.

Her sister Henrietta died in 1880. The following year, when Isabella was fifty, she married a doctor ten years her junior. He died only five years later. Isabella died in Edinburgh, Scotland, after seventy-three years of vigorous life.

*   *   *

Many a girl from the civilized East went to the frontier West, not as a settler but following the flag, as an Army wife. For such women there was no hope of a permanent home unless their husbands lived long enough to retire from the Army on a pension. They faced tedium, discomfort, danger, and sometimes imminent death, but they felt that it was better to go along with their husbands than to be separated for years.

One of these women was Elizabeth Bacon Custer. She was born in Michigan in 1842. At twenty she was valedictorian of the graduating class of a "female seminary"—that is, a boarding school—and two years later she married a handsome young Army officer with curly blond hair.

George Armstrong Custer had been graduated from the United States Military Academy just at the outbreak of the

Civil War. His bravery in action brought him one promotion after another. In 1863, when he was only twenty-four, he was a brigadier general. Later he was brevetted major general, but after the war he resumed his regular rank of captain. A brevet rank was a promotion (with no increase in pay) conferred as an honor for distinguished service.

When the Seventh Cavalry was formed to fight Indians on the frontier, Custer became its lieutenant colonel, a two-step promotion from captain. His wife always spoke of him as "the General," no matter what his current rank was.

After five years in Kansas, the Seventh was ordered to Dakota Territory in 1873. Headquarters would be at Fort Abraham Lincoln, a few miles from the present site of Mandan, South Dakota.

When the orders came, Elizabeth hurried to look at a map. Their new post was so far from civilization that she felt she was moving to Lapland.

She found that Fort Lincoln was a town complete in itself. The soldiers lived in barracks, and there were seven houses for officers. The post had a granary, a guardhouse, storehouses, stables for six hundred horses, quarters for the laundresses (wives of enlisted men), a store with a billiard room attached, a barber shop, and even a cabin for a resident photographer.

Entertainment on an isolated post was home grown. The enlisted men constructed a building for a theater and gave home-talent entertainments with sputtering, smoking candles in tin cans for footlights.

The companies took turns during the winter in giving balls in the barracks, after removing the bunks. Officers and their ladies joined the square dancing. There were few women. Refreshments sometimes included a treat of potato salad flavored with onions, which were very rare in Dakota.

Fanny Kelly

The only picture ever taken of Cynthia Ann Parker. Her baby daughter, Prairie Flower, died in infancy.

Famous Comanche warrior chief Quanah Parker was Cynthia Ann's son. Like many Indians of his time, he wore his long braids wrapped in fur.

An old woodcut of the two little German girls. Though they look fat and sassy as presented by this artist, they were pitifully scrawny when rescued from the Cheyennes.

A Sioux woman and her children in mourning in 1884. Their hair has been cut and the tepee is smaller than normal. It was the Ogallala Sioux who captured Fanny Kelly in 1864.

Library of Congress

Historical Society of Montana, Helena

The two older German sisters, shortly after they were rescued in 1875. Catherine is on the left, Sophia on the right.

One of the first women to cross the continent, Mary Richardson Walker traveled two thousand miles on horseback in 1838.

Oregon Historical Society

Sister Mary of the Infant Jesus, of the Sisters of Charity of Providence, pictured after years of dedicated service.

Mrs. Wilbur Fisk Sanders, born Harriet Fenn, went west in 1863.

Historical Society of Montana, Helena

Oxen and covered wagons on the move. Harriet Sanders traveled by wagon train from Omaha.

Historical Society of Montana, Helena

A Concord "mud wagon." Note the "boot" in the back for luggage. The Sanders family returned east for a visit by stagecoach in 1866.

Dr. Bethenia Owens-Adair

From the Nellie Cornelius Collection

Elizabeth Custer

Historical Society of Montana, Helena

General and Mrs. George Armstrong Custer in his study at Fort Lincoln. Note the portrait of General Custer on the wall and the Rogers Groups on the table.

Historical Society of Montana, Helena

Many women rode west on sidesaddles. Bethenia Owens-Adair and Isabella Bird were among the first to rebel against this custom. Note identifying brands on the horse's hip.

Sitting Bull. This is a reproduction of the oil portrait painted by
Catherine Weldon. Note the tear on the left made by bayonet.

Nannie Alderson on her eightieth birthday at a fancy dress party.

A log house and barn on a Montana ranch. Most log cabins were only half this size.

Butter churn

The kitchen used to be the activity center of the home because the stove warmed it. It was the place to eat, rock the baby, do the laundry, take a bath. Note child's bathtub, coffee pot and kettle, Dutch oven on floor with depression in lid to hold coals for cooking.

TOP RIGHT: In its day, this washing machine was a great convenience. The handle works a plunger that forces water through the clothes. For really soiled garments, a washboard was used, too.

BOTTOM RIGHT: An iron stove was a great improvement over a fireplace for cooking, heating water and irons, and warming a room. Here are a flatiron (sometimes called a sadiron), a tailor's iron for use on long seams in heavy fabrics, and a trivet or rest for the hot flatiron. Hot iron handles had to be held with thick pot holders to prevent burned fingers.

Photographs on this page and opposite page were taken at the Caroline Mc-Gill Museum at Montana State University at Bozeman by Bertha Clow.

Grace McCance Snyder

A sod house, made from
chunks of the prairie, was a
first home for many pio-
neers. Grace Snyder lived in
one.

Historical Society of Montana, Helena

The Custers had hardly finished arranging their quarters when, one bitter-cold night, the house burned down. Some things were saved by the soldiers who came running to help, but most of Mrs. Custer's clothes, silver, and linen were destroyed. The loss she really mourned was a collection of newspaper clippings about her husband. The Custers moved into another house temporarily.

Mail reached the fort seldom—it was brought by wagon for 250 miles across a trackless waste of snow. The whole post went wild with excitement when the mail came, with a half-frozen sergeant driving half-frozen mules. Trains didn't run in the winter, and the telegraph line was often broken down.

"A woman on the frontier is so cherished and appreciated," Mrs. Custer recollected, "because she has the courage to live out there, that there is nothing that is not done for her if she be gracious and courteous."

The women at Fort Abraham Lincoln were thoroughly spoiled. The officers buttoned their wives' shoes, wrapped them up if they were going out of doors, and warmed their clothes before a fire. The wives, too, made great efforts to keep their husbands happy, because they would be separated soon enough—perhaps forever—when the campaign against the Indians began in the spring.

The Custers spent all their free time together. Elizabeth's sewing chair was beside her husband's desk, and he read aloud a great deal. He was especially interested in the career of Napoleon Bonaparte. The General also wrote several articles for publication in eastern magazines, and his wife was very proud of him.

In the spring, two very frightening events occurred. Elizabeth and her husband were out riding, not far from the fort, when they found the mutilated corpse of a white man whom the Indians had killed.

Later, Indians attacked the mule herd and drove off several hundred of the animals, which were needed to haul the regiment's supply wagons. In the resulting excitement, almost every man on the post rode off to chase the Indians, leaving the women alone, unprotected, and scared half to death.

Two of the women stayed on the porch to watch for attacking Indians who might be creeping through the gulleys. Others took turns watching through a window at the back of the Custers' house. The waiting women were less terrified of death than of the horrors of capture. They remembered all the gruesome stories they had heard. They knew that the wives of military men would be more terribly treated than women captured from a peaceful settlement or from a wagon train.

Mrs. Custer and the others seriously discussed their potential ability to load a carbine. None of them knew anything about firearms.

The only men left on the post were a few troopers on guard and one officer, who kept assuring the women that everything would be all right, but they almost drove him crazy with anxious questions that he could not answer.

Late in the afternoon they saw dust on the horizon. Some of the mules were coming, driven by a few troopers—who didn't know what was happening to the rest of the regiment. The women were too worried to eat. None of the soldiers had taken any rations, and some had not even had breakfast before they galloped off.

Then, in the stillness of the evening, they heard a welcome sound: the regimental band playing the Seventh Cavalry's famous marching tune, "Garryowen."

The fort was full of groaning, limping men the following day, their muscles aching after the long, desperate ride, for they had not been in the saddle all winter. The officer who had remained at the fort maintained that they were a lot luckier than he was.

There was only one tree on their side of the river, and much as everyone longed to sit in its shade, nobody did. The Plains Indians customarily disposed of their dead by wrapping up the bodies and fastening them up in trees instead of burying them. The branches of that one held seventeen Indian corpses!

Both officers and men planted gardens that spring. The general himself enthusiastically wielded a hoe. Just when everybody was getting set for young, fresh vegetables, a cloud of grasshoppers swooped down and ate up all their dreams. A rare treat at the fort was a common cabbage. Once in a long time the Custers were able to buy one in Bismarck for a dollar and a half.

Vegetables came out of cans. So did milk. Eggs were powdered, with yolks and whites mixed together. Recipes calling for eggs and cream exasperated every cook. One frontier cook's recipe for waffles went this way: "Eggs just as you has 'em; a sprinkling of flour as you can hold in your hand; milk—well, according to what you has."

Still, adjusting to "what you has," the Custers lived very well. They had several Negro servants, one of whom boasted, "Miss Libby and I could keep house in a barrel." The Negroes were lonely for their friends back home, but they were loyal to the Custers.

Other officers' wives didn't fare so well. White women were so scarce that it wasn't possible to keep servants, even if they were old and ugly—the sergeants came courting. The wife of the commanding officer at Fort Sully told Mrs. Custer about her problems in trying to keep a governess for her children. Her last four governesses had married officers.

The Seventh included seven or eight hundred men, with

their horses—which were very well cared for, because a cavalryman's life depended on his mount. Infantry regiments, the slogging foot soldiers, moved out after Indians early in the spring, but the cavalry didn't go until later, the Army's idea being that a man could endure more hardship than a horse should be required to risk.

When the Seventh rode out in the spring, Elizabeth went along. Custer was bitterly criticized by his superiors back in Washington for taking her, not because of the danger to her but because the presence of a woman might slow the movement of the regiment in its pursuit of enemy Indians.

Elizabeth was well aware of this criticism. Determined never to hamper the movement of the troops, she taught herself never to admit that she was too hot or too cold, never to think of hunger if the regiment could not stop to eat, never to ask for a drink of water between meals. Water was scarce on the march. Years later, when she lived in New York where it was plentiful, she couldn't break the habit of using it frugally.

She wore a long, full skirt and rode sidesaddle. She was always glad to have a chance to dismount and stretch the cramps out of her muscles.

The Custers had all possible comforts on the march. (The General even took along most of his forty hunting dogs!) They had camp chairs with leather backs and seats, because when you're tired, you want something to lean against. Their bed was easy to pack in the wagon. It consisted of two saw horses with three boards laid on them.

In the evening, in camp, the General read a great deal, and his wife embroidered or mended their clothes. As they rested, they listened to the sounds of the regiment: a soldier practicing bugle calls; the click of currycombs as the troopers groomed their horses; the braying of protesting mules; the

Negro servants singing as they worked—and always melodies played on an accordion. No matter how strict the rules were or how limited the space for soldiers' baggage, somebody always managed to sneak an accordion into a wagon.

The Custers had a small stove for their sleeping tent, and sometimes evenings on the prairie were so cold that half a dozen officers would come to pay their respects—and to warm up. The Sibley stove was very simple—a cone of sheet iron, open at top and bottom. Elizabeth never ceased to wonder how so simple a thing could be so wonderfully useful.

The warmth and shelter of the tent also attracted Custer's numerous stag hounds. They crowded in, especially if there was rain, and their shaggy coats steamed odorously. Mrs. Custer had to step delicately in crossing the floor to avoid hurting feet or tails, and she was lucky if she could find a place to sit on her own bed, because the dogs usually got there first. The general always had some special plea for some special dog, with very sound reasons why that one just had to be in the nice warm tent.

More than once, Mrs. Custer was in danger from the Indians. Then she was in double jeopardy. Her husband and the other officers had absolutely agreed that rather than let her be captured by Indians, *the soldier nearest to her would shoot her without fail.* She was always uncomfortably aware, when she and her escorts encountered enemy Indians, that if one little thing went wrong, somebody—perhaps her own husband—would kill her.

Elizabeth Custer wrote, after describing a close call she had, "The next day the general thought I might rather not be with him than run the risk of such frights; but I well knew there was something far worse than fears for my own personal safety. It is infinitely worse to be left behind, a prey to all the horrors of imagining what may be happening to one we love."

The Custers returned to Fort Lincoln, where they lived in their new house built to replace the one that had burned. It was good and big, as it needed to be, for the commanding officer had to do considerable entertaining. But space was about all it had. The walls were neither painted nor papered, and the windows had to be opened by sheer brute strength. There were no window shades. Each room had its own heating stove.

The finest thing about the house was that the General at last had a room where he could work undisturbed at his writing and studying. This room, the library, was decorated with dozens of his hunting trophies—heads of a buffalo, a grizzly bear, several antelopes, a black-tailed deer. There were stuffed birds—a sand-hill crane, a mountain eagle, a great white owl—and two foxes. From racks of antlers hung the general's saber, spurs, riding whips, field glasses. His many rifles and pistols were in a stand in a corner.

The Custers always took with them two small statuettes of a kind called "Rogers Groups," which were fashionable home decorations then and are precious museum pieces now. These were little statues that told a story, not great works of art but pleasant to have around. One of the Custers' Rogers Groups, called "Letter Day," showed a soldier writing a letter home and very puzzled about what to say. These statuettes usually got some bits broken off in moving, no matter how carefully they were packed, and Custer mended them himself with putty, but not very well. Once when he put the head back on the soldier, he produced a noticeable goiter.

The new house had a long piazza, where the officers' ladies congregated in the evening. The mosquitoes at the fort were a perfect plague, ravenous and beyond counting. The ladies had to wear net bags over their heads to protect their faces, and they wrapped newspapers around their legs under the stockings and tucked their long skirts around all this. Add coats and gloves, and they were protected as long as they didn't move.

One of the social problems at the fort was that the number of officers' wives was small, and they had nobody but each other for company when the regiment was away. They did not dare quarrel! They *had* to get along together—or have no companionship at all.

In the second spring of the Custers' stay at Fort Lincoln, a pitiful thing happened. A deputation of Sioux Indians came to beg for food for the tribe. The supplies the government had promised them had not reached them the previous fall, because the steamboat stayed frozen in the river ice. The Indians had suffered greatly from starvation and had eaten their dogs and many horses.

General Custer was very well disposed toward the Indians who had consented to settle on reservations. When the tribal spokesman charged that the Indians' own agents, employed by the United States Government, were cheating them, Custer was anxious that the Army should give them some supplies to allay their hunger. Accordingly, he telegraphed the Secretary of War.

But the War Department wasn't responsible for treaty Indians; the Department of the Interior was. Permission was refused because for the War Department to hand out food that should come from another department would complicate things in Washington!

The hungry Indians knew that something called "the government" was supposed to supply their food. They couldn't understand this red-tape nonsense at all. More and more of the disgusted, desperate "friendlies" left their reservations and joined the wandering "hostiles" on the plains. Relations between Indians and whites became worse.

In the fall of 1875, General and Mrs. Custer went back to the States and spent most of the winter in New York, going to many parties, plays, and concerts. As far as one can tell from reading what Mrs. Custer wrote about this, the trip was simply for pleasure. She did not care to tell about a scandalous government investigation in which her husband was involved, against his will, as a witness before a Congressional committee.

By no means everyone admired George Armstrong Custer as his wife did. One of those who detested him was the President of the United States, Ulysses S. Grant, whose administration was riddled with scandal.

There were scandals concerning railroads and retroactive pay increases for Congressmen and the executive branch. Grant's private secretary was involved in a fraud about whisky. The President's brother, Orvil, made large sums of money by "influence peddling," just because he *was* the President's brother. Impeachment proceedings were instituted against the Secretary of War, W. W. Belknap. During the hearing that resulted in these proceedings, General Custer was summoned to testify before an investigating committee of Congress.

Belknap was accused of selling licenses to men who wanted to run trading posts on Indian reservations and army installations. A post trader, and nobody else, was entitled to sell supplies to Indians and soldiers. Many of them charged outrageous prices. Only one trading post could legally be operated by any one man, but Orvil Grant ignored this regulation and held four of them himself. The traders there divided their big profits with him.

Great quantities of supplies, which should have been

handed out to the friendly tribes of Indians as part of the treaty obligation of the federal Government, were shipped instead to other places to be sold. Some traders paid a thousand dollars a month for the privilege of handling such goods, and the illegal profits were divided between President Grant's brother and Secretary Belknap's wife. Meanwhile, the friendly Indians went hungry.

General Custer was furious at the way the soldiers and the Indians were being cheated, but he certainly did not want to risk his military career by telling what he knew. He was forced to do so, however—and President Grant found a way to get even with him for exposing the scandal. Grant saw to it that Custer's official permission to leave Washington was delayed—just when the General wanted most earnestly to return to Fort Lincoln. It was his great ambition to head the Army's great expedition against the hostile Indians.

Grant finally let him go, at the urgent request of high military officers who needed him in the campaign, but Custer was not, as he had hoped and expected, in command of the whole Dakota Column. He was relegated to a less important role.

On the morning of May 17, the Seventh Cavalry rode out from Fort Lincoln, this time not simply to police the plains but in the expectation of real fighting with the hostiles who refused to sign treaties and settle down on reservations.

About twelve hundred men moved out—soldiers, civilians employed as teamsters, and friendly Indians who were hired as scouts. Seventeen hundred horses and mules carried them and their provisions. When the band struck up "The Girl I Left Behind Me," Elizabeth Custer and the other women who were being left behind tried to smile as they waved good-by.

Fort Lincoln was not left entirely undefended. It needed

every soldier who was left there. The fort was attacked several times by roving bands of hostile Indians, and often a long roll of the drums called out the soldiers before dawn to defend the garrison.

On Sunday afternoon, June 25, 1876, the women met at the Custer home and sang hymns. Some of them burst into tears when they began to sing "Nearer, my God, to Thee."

On that same afternoon, at the Battle of the Little Bighorn, in southern Montana, General Custer and five troops of the Seventh, some 225 men in all, were slaughtered to the last man.

The terrible news did not reach Fort Abraham Lincoln until July 5.

"This battle," Mrs. Custer wrote, "wrecked the lives of twenty-six women at Fort Lincoln, and orphaned children of officers and soldiers joined their cry to that of their bereaved mothers."

Historians still wonder, in book after book, just what happened on that grim day of battle. Did Custer disobey the orders he had received from his superiors? Did his subordinate officers—at least one of whom hated him—disobey the orders he gave them? Whose fault was that shocking defeat at the Little Bighorn?

Custer has been called a glory hunter; he has been criticized for attacking a great village of hostile Sioux and Cheyenne Indians after his Crow scouts warned him they were there. He has been ardently defended, too.

It is not true that the entire Seventh Cavalry was wiped out at the Little Bighorn. Custer had five troops with him when he rode toward that stream, and all of these were killed, with not a single man left to tell what happened. But he had divided his command that morning and had sent some of his men out on two other expeditions. One force, under Captain Fred Benteen, was ordered to ride over the hills looking for Indians. The other, led by Major Marcus Reno, was following Custer's own group. Reno's men fought a bitter battle of their own and might have been wiped out if Benteen's men, returning from the hills, had not joined them.

So there were survivors who might have been able to tell something about what orders Custer really gave that morning. But his widow defended his memory all her life, and it was a very long life. She was only two days short of ninety-one when she died in New York City on April 6, 1933.

As a result of the debacle at the Little Bighorn, Major Reno was called before a military court of inquiry—not a court-martial, but an investigative body appointed to find out facts. Major Reno was accused of cowardice. He was exonerated but later was cashiered from the Army on other charges that had no connection with that battle.

Almost everything that is known about the battle is in the testimony before the court of inquiry, but historians still wonder whether some facts about Custer's own command decisions may have been covered up.

During all the fifty-six years of her widowhood, Elizabeth Custer crusaded to keep her husband's memory untarnished. Several times she took action to prevent the publication of material that might have been derogatory. The survivors who might have been able to tell something about what really happened kept silent gallantly, for the sake of Custer's widow.

When she died, only one of them was left—and he had nothing to say.

For Elizabeth Custer, her husband could do no wrong.

He was a shining hero, without a shadow of reproach, and she was determined that the world should remember him that way. History may have lost something because of this, but she was a brave and loyal wife.

8

Some Were Idealists

❦

Catherine Weldon

CATHERINE WELDON is a shadowy figure in the history of the frontier. We know of her first as a middle-aged widow traveling westward all alone from her safe, comfortable home in Brooklyn, New York, on a mission that was doomed to failure. We hear of her later when, consumed with grief, she was thinking of entering a convent. She was a brave and gallant woman.

Mrs. Weldon was a member of the National Indian Defense Association, an organization of people in the civilized eastern part of the United States who sympathized with the Indians and wanted to help them. As a representative of the N.I.D.A., she went to the Sioux Indian reservations in South Dakota in the spring of 1889, to try to help the Sioux keep the lands that the Government had given them. She had no very clear idea of the situation she would encounter on this quixotic undertaking. She simply wanted to give help and advice to the great chief, Sitting Bull, who was trying to persuade his people not to let their land be sold to non-Indians.

Sitting Bull was born in March, 1831; therefore, when

Mrs. Weldon met him, he was fifty-eight years old. He was a great leader of his people, a brave warrior, a good hunter, a medicine man—and an implacable hater of the white man's ways.

In his youth, his people lived off the great herds of buffaloes on the western plains, and they lived very well. They had plenty of horses, plenty of food, plenty of furs and tanned skins for clothing and bedding, comfortable tepees for houses. The land was theirs for farther than they could see.

But in 1889 they were a defeated people, hungry and bewildered by the white man's demands. For three years they had not hunted buffalo, because white hunters had killed the vast herds, selling the hides and wasting countless tons of good rich meat. The Sioux were dependent on rations received from the Government through agents who sometimes cheated them. In addition, the white men now wanted land that had been given by treaty to the Indians to occupy forever.

Sitting Bull stoutly opposed treaties ceding reservation lands to the whites. He had succeeded in getting the price increased on thirteen million acres by traveling to Washington, D.C., to argue about it. In 1889 another Government land commission came to the Sioux, and by trickery Sitting Bull was kept out of the deliberations.

When Catherine Weldon went to help him, another commission was trying to get more land. The Sioux had not received any payment yet—and their food rations had been cut by one-fifth! Many Indians died of starvation. The death rate among children was terribly high. The Sioux were cursed by epidemics, and they had not been able to raise a crop on their farms for three years.

It was an explosive situation into which the Brooklyn widow confidently walked! About the first thing she did was to get into a furious argument with Major James McLaughlin, the Indian agent at Standing Rock. McLaughlin (called Major because that title was usually bestowed on Indian agents) had tried his best to break Sitting Bull's power by appointing other chiefs—but the stubborn, wily old man was still the acknowledged leader of the Sioux.

When Mrs. Weldon arrived at Standing Rock, McLaughlin told her that Sitting Bull was selfish and a coward, a man of no importance. Mrs. Weldon hadn't mentioned him at all. McLaughlin had obviously intercepted and read her letters!

Sitting Bull was sick, and he was in mourning for a beloved daughter, but he drove forty miles to meet Catherine Weldon. She moved into his cabin with his three wives and acted as his secretary, writing letters for him. She began painting a full-length portrait of him in his buckskin costume and feathered head-dress. She learned the Sioux language.

She wanted him to go with her on a business trip to another agency, taking along his family in the wagon, but he was not allowed to leave his own reservation without a pass, which McLaughlin refused to issue.

Catherine lost her temper. "Are you afraid of a woman and a woman's influence?" she demanded of McLaughlin. She threatened to report him to Washington, D.C. Then she walked indignantly out of his office and left the reservation.

The white settlers desperately feared the hostile Sioux and therefore bitterly hated them. Especially they feared the power of Sitting Bull, who stubbornly and consistently stood up for the rights of his people. He had been one of the leaders of the Indians who wiped out Custer's Seventh Cavalry at the Battle of the Little Bighorn in 1876. He had then taken his people to refuge in Canada, where they remained until they were forced to return to the United States in 1881.

Most of the other Sioux chiefs had acknowledged that the United States Government had defeated them, but Sitting Bull never gave up, even after he was confined to a reservation and his band of Sioux was starving.

We can look back now, from a safe distance in time, and say, "This was a great man." But his contemporaries could not, because he was dangerous. Sitting Bull's power *had* to be broken. Many of his own Sioux people hated him as much as the whites did.

The arrival of Catherine Weldon, who announced that she wanted to help this man in his struggle with the government, was a shock to everyone who opposed him. But they found a weapon to attack Mrs. Weldon. The weapon was the sneer.

Lying, scandalous stories began to circulate about her. They were helped along by Major McLaughlin's part-Indian wife, who especially detested old Sitting Bull. The *Bismarck Daily Tribune* published a news story with these headlines:

She Loves Sitting Bull

A New Jersey Widow Falls Victim to Sitting Bull's Charms

Mrs. Weldon was, of course, hurt and angry. She blamed McLaughlin for circulating such stories, which were as untrue as the statement that she was from New Jersey. The *Sioux City Herald* even printed a story that she had come from New York to marry the old chief.

The following April, she humbled herself to the extent of writing to Major McLaughlin, hoping that he would extend her "the courtesy of a gentleman to a lady" and answer some questions.

"It is such a brave, noble deed," she wrote bitterly, "for a strong powerful man (created to protect woman) to trample upon, to annihilate woman."

Poor Catherine Weldon, falling back on that argument while refusing to adhere to the accepted rule that woman's place was in the home!

She asked McLaughlin whether she could get a claim or stay on the reservation; she wanted to build a house and give instruction in "useful domestic accomplishments" to Indian women and girls.

That summer she went west again, this time taking her only child, her son Christie, not quite fourteen. Mrs. Weldon moved in with Sitting Bull's family again, continued as the old chief's secretary, writing letters for him to other Indians and translating documents for him, washed dishes, and went on painting his portrait.

She heard disquieting rumors: the Sioux were adopting a strange new religion. For once, Catherine Weldon agreed with Major McLaughlin and other white authorities: the so-called "Ghost Dance" was dangerous and should be stopped. Down in Nevada, a Paiute Indian named Wovoka had told a few other Indians that he had visions. No doubt he believed this himself; he was a very strange person. But there were many visionaries among the Indians, and this was much easier for them to believe than it would be for us. Wovoka held out to them what seemed like their last hope for survival.

He claimed, and probably believed, that he was the Messiah. He said, "A long time ago I came to save the white people, but they killed me. This time I have come to help the Indians against the whites. I have come to save the Indians."

He taught his followers a slow ceremonial dance, with songs to be chanted, and he promised that Indians who believed in him would be saved when a great flood of mud came to cover all the white men. Then the old days would come again—the old days of freedom, with plenty of horses and vast buffalo herds. All the Indians would be together again, the living and their loved ones who had died.

All this would happen very soon, he said. Sometimes in the slow, solemn dance a man (but more often a mourning woman) lost consciousness and went into a kind of hypnotic trance, to tell later of having talked to the dead. Therefore it was called the Ghost Dance.

News of all this spread like prairie fire. The faraway Sioux sent some of their wisest old men to investigate. They believed, and they returned to the reservations to teach the Ghost Dance and the songs.

A Sioux named Kicking Bear was the chief exponent of the new religion. Mrs. Weldon did everything she could to stop its spread, but she was helpless. The Sioux had to believe in something—and the white men had ordered them, in 1886, to stop their ancient springtime ceremony of the Sun Dance, which was a mystic renewal of the spirit of the whole tribe. (Not until 1934 were the Indians permitted to revive the Sun Dance. You can still see it on some reservations.)

Mrs. Weldon wrote to McLaughlin: "I have every reason to believe that five tribes are ready to fight. It is heart-rending to see how zealous they are in their faith of this false Christ, and reject the true Christ about whom I spoke to all the Indians, explaining our faith. They believe that some terrible fate will overtake me for my sacrilegious utterances against their Christ. Poor misguided beings, so earnestly desiring to seek God, groping blindly for the true light and not finding it. If I had known what obstinate minds I had to contend with, I would not have undertaken this mission to enlighten and instruct them. It was money, health and heart thrown away."

It was, indeed. Her son Christie stepped on a nail just

before she started back home in November, 1890. The foot
got better, but on the Missouri River steamer *Chaska,* lock-
jaw set in. He died after terrible suffering while the boat
was stuck on a sandbar near Pierre, South Dakota, before a
doctor could be reached.

"He did not like to die," Mrs. Weldon wrote to Sitting
Bull from Kansas City, Missouri, "but clung to life and to
me for day and night. I could not leave his side and held his
hands until he died. I took his body on shore and left the
boat at Pierre. Put him in a coffin and an extra box and took
him with me to this place, Kansas City. Last Monday the
seventeenth we buried him here.

"All this extra expense has made me *poor.* You know that
I told you I was no longer rich. Now I have nothing more
to live for. Away from the Dakotas, my boy gone forever,
what is there left for me? . . . Remember my boy! He was the
only son of your best friend; mourn for him." She signed
herself Toka Heya Mani Win, her Sioux name, meaning
"Woman Walking Ahead."

Three days later, November 23, she wrote again to Sitting
Bull on black-bordered stationery. She had thought she
might go back to the Sioux and be killed with them; she had
given up the idea of suicide because her religious faith did
not permit it, but she had spoken to a priest about the idea
of becoming a nun. He had advised her to do nothing rash.

She told Sitting Bull, "I wish you would try to live an
honest, noble life and do what is right in the eyes of God,
and let your heart be true to those who deserve it, that when
death comes to both of us we may not be eternally separated
but meet again in a better world. I have made great sacrifices
for you and your people."

She wrote again, still despairing, on December 1. Various
newspapers were still telling lies about her and even blaming

her for the Ghost Dance and the threatened outbreak of the Sioux. And she had lost all her possessions—books, two paintings of Sitting Bull, her letters and valuable documents, her silverware, and all the beautiful Indian things she had collected.

These letters were found in Sitting Bull's cabin after he was dead. He was killed December 15 by Indian police whom the white authorities had sent to arrest him. Another thing that was found was Catherine Weldon's full-length oil portrait of him, bearing her signature, C. S. Weldon, in one corner.

Fifteen days after the murder of Sitting Bull, white soldiers fired on a camp of frightened Sioux at Wounded Knee Creek and killed about three hundred men, women and children. After that massacre, the Ghost Dance religion collapsed.

9

Some Lived Far from Town

Nannie Alderson and Grace Snyder

SOME OF THE WOMEN who went west were accustomed to constant hard work and making do. A move from a rented farm that produced little above the bare subsistence level to free land, rich land in the West was, for such women, an improvement in living. They took with them their household skills and their memorized recipes.

But for women like Nannie Alderson, who had never worked, the change was a jolting one. She grew up in the South—a South shattered by defeat in the Civil War but still with its old, gracious traditions and customs. Her grandmother's home in West Virginia, where she was reared, had Negro servants, no longer slaves but with a long history of loyalty to the family. Nannie went as a bride to a raw, new country where there were no servants. Women were few, and they lived far apart. There was no casual visiting back and forth. There was bright hope for prosperity, but the bright hope faded.

Nannie Tiffany was born in 1860. Her father, a captain in the Confederate Army, was killed in the First Battle of Manassas when she was a baby. Her mother married again, and thereafter Nannie lived with her grandmother. She attended public school and later learned a little music and a little French in a seminary for girls, but her schooling ended when she was fifteen.

She spent most of the next year with an aunt in Atchison, Kansas. That seemed Way Out West, and she found customs there very different from those back home. A nice girl could even work in a store, although Nannie wasn't allowed to do so. Life was informal in Atchison—ladies took their darning or knitting when they went visiting. Later, when Nannie tried this back home in West Virginia, her female relatives were horrified.

On this first visit to Atchison, she met a cowboy wearing a big hat and spurs, a man with an aura of romance about him. Walt Alderson had run away to Texas when he was about twelve, and during Nannie's visit he returned for the first time, as a member of a crew of cowboys driving a trail herd of Longhorn cattle.

On a later visit to her aunt's home, Nannie met him again. He was half an inch under six feet tall, blue-eyed and handsome. He planned to go to Montana to set up in the cattle business, and he confidently expected to get rich. This time when he and Nannie parted, they were engaged to be married. Nannie spent the next year in West Virginia making her trousseau. Her wedding dress was of white embroidered mull, and she earned the money to buy her wedding veil by making a dress for the wife of a freed slave of her grandfather's, a Negro woman for whom the professional dressmakers in the community refused to sew.

Nannie Tiffany and Walt Alderson were married at her mother's house on April 4, 1883. Then they set out on the railroad for the great open spaces and a kind of life that the bride had not known existed.

In Miles City, Montana, they bought supplies to be freighted by wagon to the ranch, one hundred miles away. One item was a bottle of "starter" for making yeast. One night when they were sound asleep, there was a loud crack like a pistol shot right in their hotel room. Walt grabbed his six-gun—and then discovered that the yeast had popped the cork out of the bottle.

The nearest thing to a motel in those days was a road ranch—simply a ranch house where the family took in travelers for pay. The Aldersons stayed at one road ranch where they were lucky enough to have a room all to themselves. The bunk room had fifteen men in it, all talking about the money they were going to make raising cattle and horses.

The Aldersons' first home, while their own log house was being built, was a dirt-roofed log cabin with one door and one window. Over the door hung an immense pair of elk antlers supporting a human skull full of bullet holes. Nobody knew whose it was—the skull was just a decoration.

Walt's ranching partner, John Zook, and the cowboys on the place had done their best to prepare the cabin for occupancy by a lady—they had taken the pictures of actresses off the walls, built a fire in the stone fireplace, and spread a sheet of white canvas on the dirt floor. Mountain lion, wolf, coyote, and fox pelts were laid on the canvas for scatter rugs.

The backyard "convenience" had no roof, for a peculiar reason. It was made of boards, standing on end, and lumber was so expensive that the hired hand who built it refused to "waste" any of the material by sawing off the uneven ends. It wasn't possible to put a roof on the little building, because the boards stuck up in the air to various heights, so the top remained open to the rain and snow.

Nannie hadn't learned to cook at home. She learned from her husband and the hired cowboys. All cowboys could cook

—they had to learn or starve to death. The table was crude, and there were rough benches instead of chairs, but the bride used her grandmother's silver with a lazy Susan as a decorative centerpiece. A lazy Susan was a silver stand that held glass salt and pepper shakers and cruets for vinegar and mustard. It revolved at a touch so these things didn't have to be passed around.

Laundry was a serious problem. So was loneliness. For more than three months Nannie didn't see a white woman except a disagreeable neighbor four miles away who let her daughter-in-law do the washing but not the ironing. Nannie sighed for Aunt Rose, the Negro laundress back home in West Virginia. Then she did the washing herself—with all sorts of sad results. The water in that area is very alkaline, and white clothing and linens came out yellow, with gummy black balls of alkali that stuck to the hot flatiron. The cowboys stretched a lariat for a clothesline—and the wind blew the wet clothes off the line onto the sawdust in the yard.

Getting a washing done was a problem everywhere except in a few big cities where commercial laundries had been established. Many California gold miners, in the Days of '49, sent their dirty clothes all the way to the Sandwich Islands (Hawaii) by sailing ship!

On the ranch, young Mrs. Alderson found that the dresses she had brought along were anything but suitable. She had a black silk dress, a dark blue one with lots of pretty ruffles on the skirt, and a white poplin one trimmed with broad black velvet bands. They all had stylish trains, and there was no canvas on the dirt floor of the kitchen. She also had a sensible blue serge, but the dirt roof leaked after a heavy snow storm (in May!) and ruined it.

She tried to keep the others fresh by tucking pieces of her wedding veil into the necks. Dry cleaning had been invented in Paris in 1849, but there were few dry-cleaning establishments in the United States, and they were in the major cities. As recently as 1945, many American families still did their own dry cleaning at home with gasoline.

Nannie Alderson had no coat hangers, so garments had to be hung on nails—not the best way to keep them in shape. She wore high black buttoned shoes, but no shoe polish had been brought along with the supplies.

Anything that was forgotten on the annual trip to Miles City, a hundred miles away, had to be done without. When the men went there in the fall, to ship the cattle, they bought supplies to last for a year. Everything except meat, milk, and butter (and, later, a few home-grown vegetables) had to come that way. Flour and sugar were purchased in hundred-pound sacks; there were whole sides of bacon, cases of canned goods, great quantities of dried fruit, huge tins of coffee.

When Walt's work pants wore out before it was time to go to town, Nannie had to make him a pair from a gray blanket. She ripped the old ones apart to use as a pattern. She didn't think much of the way the blanket pants fit her husband, but he bragged about his wife's cleverness.

Paper patterns were among the things that were hard to get. They had been sold commercially, however, for about twenty years. Ebenezer Butterick, a tailor and shirtmaker, and his wife put a set of shirt patterns, made of stiff paper, on the market. Then Mrs. Butterick suggested patterns for children's clothes. These were cut from tissue paper so they would cost less to mail.

Now, women who make clothing for their families sew because they enjoy sewing. In the nineteenth century, women sewed because they had to. Manufacture of ready-to-wear things for women didn't begin until 1860, and nobody had much admiration for "store clothes" anyway.

Strange to say, the first factory-made clothing was for slaves in the South. They had made their own clothes until about 1840; then plantation owners found that it was more profitable to keep the slaves at work in the fields cultivating cotton and buy cheap, ready-made work clothing for them.

Invention of the sewing machine made the clothing industry possible. The first one, which used only one thread and sewed a chain stitch, was patented by a French tailor in 1830. Elias Howe, Jr., an American, patented a two-thread machine—much better—in 1844. Isaac Merrit Singer built an even better one in 1850.

Paper patterns and sewing machines—what a difference they have made!

The Aldersons' first ranch was in a pretty place, a wide valley with a creek between pine-covered hills. Wild roses grew in profusion in the spring.

Indians were always peeking into the house, but it didn't occur to Nannie yet to be afraid of them, although these were the northern Cheyennes, who had been implacable enemies of the whites until they surrendered to General Nelson Miles only two years before. One of them was Two Moons, who had been a fierce fighter in the battle of the Little Big Horn seven years earlier. This warrior had a little joke—he kept asking Walt Alderson how many horses he wanted for Nannie.

Life on the ranch was good. Nannie often left her housework to go down to the corral to watch the men break horses or brand cattle. She liked to ride, but the horses weren't used to having flapping skirts around and didn't want to be ridden anyway. So when she wanted to ride, one of the men would put her long-skirted blue riding habit on himself, and her sidesaddle on a horse, and let the bronc buck until it was tired enough to put up with any kind of nonsense. A mustached cowboy in a long skirt, sitting a sidesaddle on a bucking horse—that must have been a sight worth watching!

In the summer she was alone much of the time. The men traveled far to round up cattle, or if they were on the home place they worked all day in the hay meadows. Nannie learned to carry her own wood and water—and she learned the sound a rattlesnake makes. Her husband shot one right in the kitchen. The next morning she almost put her hand on a rattler in the stable when she was attending to a setting hen.

She learned to make butter and to care for fresh meat after butchering. She had no icebox, but the men built her a spring house fifty yards from the cabin where she could keep food cool. She picked wild plums and made preserves.

In August, the new log house was finished. It had board floors and four rooms. There was a kitchen, Johnny Zook had one room, the hired cowboys slept in a bunkroom, and the living room was also the Alderson's bedroom. The men played cards at night by the fireplace, and Nannie sewed. She was making baby clothes, but according to the custom of the time, only her husband was supposed to be aware of this fact.

Nannie Alderson never called her husband by his first name. Southern women simply never did that—servants were addressed by first names, but not husbands. Nannie did not say "Walt"; she said "Mr. Alderson." Later she dropped the formality to some extent, and she and her husband called each other "Pardsy," a nickname that evolved from "Partner."

In February, with the temperature at thirty degrees below zero, Nannie packed up for a trip of one hundred miles to Miles City to have her baby. Even now, ranchers' wives in isolated areas usually move to town to have babies—but they go in comfortable automobiles or in privately owned planes and are cared for in modern hospitals.

Walt Alderson put sled runners on a spring wagon and hitched up a team of horses. Nannie took along the things she thought she would need for a stay of four to six weeks, not guessing that she would never again see all the things she left in the new house.

Finding a place in town where she could have the baby and stay for some weeks was not easy. Only one woman was willing to take her in. During the three weeks she waited, the Yellowstone River flooded because of an ice jam, and she had to be moved temporarily to a ramshackle hotel, where her room was right over the bar.

The baby, a girl, was two days old when a telegram came for Walt Alderson: "Indians have burned your house. Come immediately with sheriff and posse."

Everything was gone—the new house, treasured possessions, even Nannie's grandmother's silver.

The reason for the Indian attack was this: The Cheyennes, now that the great buffalo herds were wiped out, were poor and hungry. Occasionally they stole a rancher's cow and butchered it for meat. A Cheyenne chief named Black Wolf came to the Alderson-Zook place one day, asked for food, was fed, and then sat down outside for a smoke.

A reckless cowboy named Hal Taliafero shot at his hat, just for fun. But Black Wolf saw nothing funny about it, and the men at the ranch could tell that trouble was coming. They rode hard for a store, ten miles away, to get rifles and men to help them defend the place, but when they returned, the ranch house was a roaring bonfire.

Everything was gone—a year's supply of groceries, Nannie's chickens, the corral, the saddles, and all the things that she had brought to make a home in the wilderness.

While the men were building a new house on a site thirty miles from the burned one, and moving the cattle to the new ranch, Nannie and the baby stayed in town at the hotel. For exercise, she took walks, carrying the baby. One day, a group of stockmen brought a baby carriage to the public parlor of the hotel and presented it to her. How she did appreciate that kindness!

Meanwhile, back on the ranch that she hadn't even seen yet, one of the men got into a squabble with an Indian who was trying to stampede the cattle, shot at him, and broke his arm. The Cheyennes were furious again. The men "forted up" inside the unfinished house, taking their horses in with them, and a messenger rode to warn the nearest neighbor. But there was no attack this time. Walt set the Indian's broken arm and made him a big present of coffee, sugar, and beef. The trouble was over.

In August, after Walt had shipped his cattle from Miles City, he took his wife and the baby, Mabel, to the new house. It was bigger than the old one, but the Aldersons never again had furniture as nice as what they had lost.

Life on the ranch was harder now, with the baby to care for. The men took turns washing dishes, but housekeeping was a burden. Nannie's standards were high, and she didn't relax them until she read in a magazine some hints written by another woman who had lived on a ranch. After that, she didn't iron baby dresses, sheets, or pillow cases.

Occasionally she had some help with the washing from an Indian woman named Rattlesnake and her sixteen-year-old daughter, Bob-Tail Horse, who was a good sitter for little Mabel. The baby's shoes had slick soles, and she kept falling on the grass until Bob-Tail Horse made her a tiny pair of skid-proof moccasins. But Nannie had learned to be afraid of Indians, and she lived with fear whenever the men had to work far from the house.

In the spring of 1886, when Mabel was two, Nannie took her back to West Virginia for a visit—and to have another baby. Mabel had a fine time on the train. She assumed that the Negro porters were Cheyenne Indians and chattered to them in the Cheyenne language. It is a very difficult language to learn, but Mabel had picked it up from the Indians.

In August, Fay Sue was born in West Virginia. Her mother didn't return to the ranch until March, 1887. Meanwhile, the cattle business in Montana had suffered a disastrous blow from a terrible winter. Some stockmen lost 90 per cent of their herds. Walt Alderson and Johnny Zook came out better than that, but their firm was deep in debt, and they were paying 18 per cent interest on money they had to borrow.

The return to the ranch from Miles City was anything but pleasant. The family traveled in an open box sled, but not very far, because a heavy snowstorm struck during their first night at a road ranch. The sled was filled with hay, covered with buffalo robes and blankets. Over it, Walt Alderson built a frame of bent willow poles and covered them with a wagon sheet. Cooped inside this, with two babies to keep pacified, Nannie traveled for four days.

A few months later, the Aldersons moved again for the third time in four years, because Walt and Johnnie Zook dissolved their partnership. This time the house had only two rooms, with two bunks in the kitchen for the cowboys. The board floors were splintery, and Fay was creeping, so Nannie made a kind of apron to hang from the baby's shoulders and protect her knees. Later, Nannie dyed the floor brown and oiled it so that it wouldn't show grease.

The new ranch was lonelier than the two before it. Few people passed that way.

With two busy little girls running around, Nannie had plenty of sewing to do, and plenty of washing. She made pinafores for both of them, of blue and white gingham tied with a sash. Every week she washed fourteen pinafores and fourteen pairs of white cambric panties. Nobody had yet invented overalls for small children or thought of making bloomers of the same material as dresses.

Sometimes there was a doctor at the Cheyenne Agency; sometimes there wasn't. Even now, on ranches in the area where Nannie Alderson lived, an injury is a serious emergency. A doctor may fly up from Sheridan, Wyoming, sixty-five miles away, charging a dollar a mile.

The Aldersons' third baby, Patty, was born on the ranch. No doctor was available, but a good neighbor, Mrs. Young, came to help.

The fourth baby was a long-awaited boy. This time, too, there was no doctor. Mrs. Alderson was cared for by a ranch cook who claimed to be a widwife but either didn't know very much or had forgotten most of it. She bathed little Walter in a cold room after she let the fire go out, and he was sick for the first three months of his life.

When Mabel was six or seven, she fell while running, hit her chin on a rock, and bit her tongue almost in two. There was no doctor, but Walt knew that Father Vandervelden, at the Catholic Mission many miles away, had studied medicine. Walt sent an Indian to ride fast for the priest, and all night he kept the little girl quiet by giving her a sip of milk whenever she cried. She was frantic with terror because she thought the tongue would have to be sewed. The priest, by riding hard, arrived after sunup. The bitten tongue did not require stitches, and it healed well.

In the summer of 1889 there was a serious Indian scare, this time among the Crows, not the Cheyennes. A medicine

man said he had had a vision that told him this was the time
for the Indians to exterminate the white people. Walt Alderson was in Nevada, buying cattle, when word of impending
danger reached the ranch, but a storekeeper took Nannie
and her children to his house for safety. The medicine man
was killed in a fight between federal troops and the Crows.

Ranch life was fine for the children. They loved watching
horses being shod and calves being branded. They treasured
various pets—two wolf pups that got away; a fawn that became dangerous with its sharp hoofs and had to be shot; two
goats; a horse named Black Wolf; and, of course, a dog, whose
name was Dude.

The children could not go to school until Mabel was almost ten, but they learned to read from the Montgomery
Ward catalogue and were entranced by the pictures in it.
Their mother taught them to print in block letters, but she
didn't tackle arithmetic.

Unless you have lived in a really isolated place, you may
not understand how important mail-order catalogues were
for rural families. The day the new catalogue came was almost as exciting as Christmas. Through its pages, farm families got almost their only glimpse of the wonderful things in
the great outside world.

Thousands of things to want, to dream about, were pictured and described in the "wish book," sometimes called
"the sheepherder's bible." The family wished and dreamed
—for a sewing machine, toys, a saddle, a dress, a new wash
tub that didn't leak. There they were, all the grand, desirable
things. You couldn't afford to buy many of them, but you
could pretend, even to the extent of making out complete
orders and mailing them—in the kitchen fire.

Montgomery Ward (affectionately known as Monkey
Ward) published a thin little eight-page catalogue in 1874.

Sears, Roebuck ("Shears Sawbuck") began in 1886. Both of them are still in business, publishing big, beautiful wish books, and in recent years they have operated retail stores, too.

The Aldersons experienced another Indian scare in the summer of 1890. A young rancher came upon some Cheyennes who were butchering a stolen steer, and they killed him. After that, whenever Walt was late in coming home, his wife worried, fearing that he had been shot and his body hidden in a coulee somewhere.

In 1893 there was a financial panic; the bank in Miles City failed, and livestock prices dropped disastrously. Walt Alderson decided to give up ranching and move his family to Miles City, where he had the promise of a job. His wife was tremendously relieved—now she could stop worrying about Indian attacks, and the children could go to school.

The job didn't materialize, but in the spring of 1894 Walt was appointed deputy county assessor, and the future looked brighter.

In March of the following year, tragedy struck. Walt was kicked in the head by a vicious horse in his own stable and died six days later without regaining consciousness.

Nannie lived in Miles City for seven more years, supporting her children by doing all kinds of work. She ran a boarding house, made bread to sell, kept a cow and sold the milk. In 1902, she took the family to a tiny settlement called Birney, a few miles from the ranches where she had lived. She opened a store, with cowboys and Indians as customers, and was postmistress.

Mabel, who had gone to high school in Miles City, married and lived on a ranch. Patty married Bill Eaton, who had a ranch near Sheridan, Wyoming. Fay taught school. Walter was a skilled cowpuncher at thirteen, drawing a man's wages.

He and his mother bought some cattle and built up a small herd, but they lost everything during another financial crash in 1919.

So, when she was sixty, Nannie Alderson went to live with her daughter Patty at Eaton's ranch, which was the first of the dude ranches. In spite of the hardships she had endured, she lived to be almost eighty-seven.

*   *   *

After the covered-wagon pioneers went west to seek their fortunes and their fates, another frontier opened up. To the vast prairies of the Dakotas and Nebraska, with their uncertain rainfall and violent storms, came the sod-shanty pioneers.

One of them, in 1885, was Grace McCance, who had no voice in her family's decision to move from Missouri to Nebraska because she was only three years old at the time. She had an older sister, Florrie, and a younger one; four more sisters and two brothers were born later.

Movers to Nebraska, by that time, traveled by railroad. Grace's father, Charles, sold his only milch cow to pay for moving everything the family owned—household goods, farm implements, three horses and a mule colt—in an "immigrant car," a railroad freight car. Mrs. McCance and the three children—only three of them then—went by passenger train.

Like most homesteaders on the Great Plains, the McCances lived in a house made of earth. The soddy was the typical first home of most people who filed for free land on the prairie. Trees were too scarce to be cut for building log cabins, and lumber was too costly, so the tough prairie sod itself was used for building material. It was cut into neat blocks, which were piled up solidly to make the thick walls. The roof, supported by planks, was made of sod, too.

Prairie homesteaders used to sing a song like this:

> Oh, the door has leather hinges
> And the window has no glass,
> And the roof it lets the howling blizzard in,
> And I hear the hungry coyote
> As he prowls along the grass
> In my little old sod shanty on the claim.
> Oh, I wish that some kind-hearted miss
> Would pity on me take
> And would extricate me from the fix I'm in.
> Oh, I would love her dearly
> If this her home she'd make,
> In my little old sod shanty on the claim.

The McCances' first "soddy" was one room only twelve by fourteen feet in size, but compared to many others it was luxurious. It had a wooden floor, and the inner walls were whitewashed. Grace's mother bleached flour sacks and embroidered them with red birds to make curtains for the three little windows.

Every drop of water for the household and the livestock had to be hauled in barrels by wagon from another homestead two miles away, where there was a well with a windmill to run the pump. Another hardship was that, having no cow or chickens at first, the family had no milk, butter, or eggs.

For a field crop, Mr. McCance raised corn. A kitchen garden provided much of the family's food—onions, beans, watermelons, and sweet corn. Mrs. McCance cut the sweet corn from the cobs, spread it on a sheet on the flat roof of the soddy, and climbed up there several times a day to turn and stir the kernels as they browned in the sun.

Dried sunflowers provided fuel for cooking and heating—
Mr. McCance laid half a dozen of the long, thick stalks together, tied them with twine, and sawed them into lengths to
fit the stove. When those were gone, the family burned corncobs and stalks. Later, when they accumulated cattle, they
burned dried cow chips, known as "prairie coal."

The little girls never had store-bought dolls, but their
mother showed them how to make dolls of corncobs, with
corn silk for hair and hats of dried sunflower heads trimmed
with chicken feathers. Grace and her older sister, Florrie, had
whole families of dolls.

The land was wonderfully fertile. Everything they planted
grew like mad. But until they got their own well dug, the
scarcity of water was a constant exasperation. The chickens
got the family bath water to drink.

Even very small children had their own work to do. Grace
and her sister had the responsibility of following their
mother's turkey hens to find where they laid their eggs in
brush or tall grass. The eggs had to be brought home to keep
skunks from eating them. When the hens turned broody
and decided to settle down and hatch their chicks, Mrs. Mc-
Cance made safe nests for them in boxes in the yard. One
turkey hen had disappeared after her chicks were hatched,
and the old gobbler mothered them under his wings and led
them around looking for food.

Grace was not yet six years old when her father assigned
her to herd the cows he had bought, keeping them out of the
cornfields. She was his boy, he said, and she was proud indeed
of the responsibility he gave her. But it was lonesome work,
and she wanted something to keep her mind and hands busy.
She begged her mother for some tiny scraps of cloth and
learned how to piece quilts. In later years, her beautiful
quilts took many prizes and made her famous.

When Grace was six and Florrie was eight, they had a chance to go to school for three months, walking three miles each way. Schools weren't permanently established—when a teacher could be found, and a room for the school, there it was, but not for very long.

Grace couldn't finish that first term; her father needed her to help plant corn. He tied a rag marker to a spoke in the right wheel of the planter. Then as he drove the team, Grace pulled the lever every time the rag came to the top of the wheel. That made the machine plant two hills of corn.

Farmers always live close to the weather. You can't do anything about weather except enjoy it or endure it, depending on what kind of weather you're having. For Nebraska homesteaders, weather seemed especially violent because there was no shelter or forest in that wide flat land.

The McCance family adjusted to the violence as well as anybody could. Blizzards—heavy snowfalls whirled by screaming winds—were a peril in the winter, and they still are, in open country. During a blizzard it wasn't safe to go out of the soddy, but it was necessary because the stock had to be fed and fuel had to be brought in for the stove. A blizzard is an utterly blinding storm in which anyone gets lost in no time, so to get from the house to the barn it was necessary to have a rope tied between the two. You can grasp a rope and grope your way along it even when you can't see a thing.

Another kind of prairie wind is the welcome chinook, which melts snow unbelievably fast so that there is rushing water everywhere. Then there is another peril: floods that wash out rickety bridges and cut off all communication.

Sometimes children in school with their teachers couldn't get home for a day or two but simply had to stay there until the snow or wind stopped or the flood water subsided. There was no way of getting word back to their homes. Everybody simply had to be patient.

Another menace on the prairie was fire, roaring through the wild grass with a howling wind whipping it on. Sometimes buildings, livestock, and even human lives were lost. Grace's father, like other homesteaders, ploughed fire guards, and these strips of raw earth with no grass on them to burn saved the family and its possessions more than once.

There was no end to the sudden dangers that weather produced. One sultry night in July, a lightning storm struck and fierce wind blew the roof off the kitchen that had been added to the sod house. Mrs. McCance had a hard time finding enough undamaged food in the mass of mud to prepare breakfast. Many things, blown out across the prairie, never were found at all. Only half of the McCances' marriage certificate, which had hung on the wall, could be found.

Grace's mother made her own yeast by boiling hop leaves with cornmeal—a mess that gave off a sickening smell—and then drying the resulting mush in hard cakes to use for making bread.

Grace went barefoot except in winter. Once she stepped on a nail, injuring her foot, and while that was healing her sister took over the chore of herding cows. Even when she couldn't walk, Grace kept busy, pounding bits of broken dishes and old buffalo bones into a grit that the chickens needed.

Grace's father finally found time to dig a well (luckily, he struck water 150 feet down). Water was brought up by mule-power. That is, one of the children would lead an old mule with a rope that pulled a rope that went over a windlass to pull the heavy bucket up from the well. Mr. McCance no longer had to waste time hauling water from two miles away, but the family still had to be careful not to waste it, because somebody had to carry all of it up a steep hill to the house.

The following year a windmill and a pump were installed so that water supply was almost at the soddy's door.

Very soon thereafter, the family moved and left the fine well behind. Mr. McCance "proved up" on his homestead; he had lived on it long enough and put enough work into it so that the land was legally his. He sold it, bought a quarter section (160 acres) and started all over.

One reason for the great migrations westward during the nineteenth century was that people wanted land for farming. There was land in plenty, thousands of square miles of it. Farmers and their families moved westward to claim it.

In 1862, President Abraham Lincoln signed the first Homestead Act, throwing vast stretches open to settlement at very low cost. Any citizen twenty-one years old could file a claim on 160 acres—a quarter section—and become eligible, after five years, to buy it for only a dollar and a quarter an acre. This was known as "proving up."

During the five years, he (or she—many homesteaders were schoolteachers) was required to cultivate a certain amount of the land and make specified improvements, such as building a dwelling. But he didn't have to live there all that time. Many homesteaders had no intention of living permanently on their land. They worked somewhere else most of the year, lived on the claim for part of the summer, paid a neighbor to make the improvements, and then sold the land at a profit if they could find a buyer.

Long before 1862, of course, settlers were moving into new areas and using the land. They gained ownership in various ways. For example, early settlers in Oregon were assured of title to the land they occupied by the Oregon Donation Act, passed in 1850, which also granted free land to newcomers who got there by 1855.

The McCances' soddy on their new farm had a bedroom, a sitting room, and a big kitchen. A Sunday School was established near enough to their new place so that the family could attend. At first, it was hard to find hymns that everyone could follow, because each family brought its own old hymn book, Methodist, Lutheran, or Christian. It was no use saying "Turn to page so-and-so," because all the books were different.

When Grace was nine, she attended school again, but only part of each day. She was needed to herd cattle mornings and afternoons, so she went to school only between recesses. One field that the children had to cross had little owls in it, and when they became cross during nesting season, the youngsters had to run while they batted the angry owls away from their faces.

That year, the McCance home got something wonderful—a new kitchen stove with an attached reservoir, a tank for heating water. As they became more prosperous, they got something else that delighted them: a washing machine. It wasn't automatic and it wasn't electric—that kind of washing machine was yet to be invented—but it certainly beat the old washboard. A three-legged "dolly" under the lid was turned back and forth by means of a handle on top, with child power, and fifteen minutes of that sloshing cleaned the whole tub full of laundry as well as if each garment had been scrubbed on a washboard.

Wash day used to be a weekly crisis. First, there was the matter of getting water into the house. Lucky the woman who had a pump in the kitchen! Usually water had to be carried in buckets from somewhere outside—and that took a lot of trips. (All the water had to be carried out again, too.)

Many families used two kinds of water. If the main supply was hard, soft water was needed for laundry. An estab-

lished household might have an underground cistern, into
which rain water ran, with a pump to bring it up. If there
was no cistern, a big barrel under the eavespout caught rain
water from the roof. It also caught leaves, weeds, bugs, and
other assorted trash, which had to be strained out.

The white clothes were usually "put to soak" Sunday night.
Early Monday morning the labor began. Doing the weekly
wash could keep a mother and several children busy. Somebody had to keep bringing in fuel for the kitchen stove. It
took a lot of fuel to heat the big wash boiler on top of the
stove. While one child lugged in wood or other fuel, another
one or two carried water to fill the boiler. A child didn't have
to be very smart to discover that it is easier to carry two
buckets than one, because this balances the weight evenly.

To loosen the dirt in the clothes, Mother scrubbed them
on the washboard, using soap that she had made herself by
boiling lye with waste fat left over from hog butchering.

When she had the skin well rubbed off her knuckles on
the washboard, she put the white clothes and some more
soap into the wash boiler and actually boiled the whole thing
for a while. This was pretty grim in hot weather, with the
heat from the stove and the steam from the boiler combin-
ing to make discomfort.

Every housewife who had ever worn out a store-bought
broom had a "clothes stick" that she prized greatly. It was a
piece of broom handle, with which she dipped the blistering
hot clothes out of the boiler. By twisting the stick, she
squeezed out as much soapy water as possible without touch-
ing the clothes.

From the boiler, the clothes went into a tub of cold water
(which warmed up soon enough), and the lady of the house
stirred them with her stick to get the soap suds out.

A second tub of rinse water was needed after that; for

white things, like sheets and shirts and dresses, this had blu-
ing added.

She couldn't just dip things out of the first rinse into the
second. She had to wring the water out of each article. And
after the second rinse, she had to wring everything again
before hanging the wash on the clothesline.

Families that weren't prosperous enough to own a clothes
boiler and two tubs had to make do with what they had, of
course.

A wonderful help was a hand wringer that could be
clamped to a tub. A child didn't have to be very big to help
Mother by turning the wringer. Youngsters developed considerable muscle this way.

With the stove top occupied by the boiler, there was little
space left for preparing noon dinner, so that was usually
something that could be cooked in the oven, which was hot
anyway from the fire in the stove.

Tuesday, ironing day, was another hot day in the kitchen.
In warm weather, ironing with an automatic electric iron can
be a fairly sweaty business even now, but before electric irons
were invented, flatirons were used. They were heated on the
stove, and several were needed, because each one cooled off
fast. Flatirons were sometimes called sad irons. You can figure out why.

The early ones were solid metal, and the handle had to be
held with a cloth pad to protect the hand from burns. While
adjusting the garment on the ironing board, the flatiron had
to be put somewhere, usually on a good thick mail-order catalogue. (The odor of scorched paper still takes many older
people back to the security and warmth of their mothers'
kitchens.)

At the same time the McCances got their child-powered

washing machines, another wonderful improvement was added. Grace's mother had done her canning in tin cans, sealing the lids on with hot sealing wax. Now she had glass jars for the first time, with lids that screwed on. They were easier to use, looked very pretty lined up on the shelves, and didn't have to be labeled. But something went wrong when Florrie canned some tomatoes all by herself while her mother was away. All the jars blew up.

Mr. McCance surprised his family one Sunday morning by appearing with a fine new spring wagon to take them to Sunday School. It was called a carryall, it had shiny black paint and two padded black patent-leather seats, and it rode on springs—altogether a handsome and comfortable vehicle, a great improvement over the jolty old wagon that had provided transportation previously.

Prosperity wasn't always with them, however. In the winter of 1894, the milch cows dried up earlier than usual because the grass was so poor, and Mrs. McCance could no longer make butter to sell. The price of eggs, which she sold, fell disastrously low, and the price of bacon, which they bought, went up.

A dreadful year of drought followed. The cattle became thin, and by the time the new little pigs were weaned there was no corn left for them. Two younger sisters now herded the cattle, while Grace and Florrie kept moving the pigs to fields where they could forage for enough shoots and stems to keep them alive.

A terrible wind storm sent the family flying to the cellar for refuge. The big granary was ruined, and the corn crib was damaged. Most of the chickens were killed. When harvest time came, there was nothing to harvest. Mr. McCance finally killed the young pigs and fed the meat to the few chickens that remained. He tried to sell his cattle, because there was no feed for them, but he couldn't even give them away, because nobody else had feed.

Nobody had any money, either. Many families gave up and moved away. And that autumn, the McCance's seventh baby was born—the first boy, and very welcome. Money was so scarce that Mr. McCance took almost two years to pay the doctor's fee of ten dollars, fifty cents or a dollar at a time.

At every social gathering, people sang a song that became very popular in those hard times:

> We've reached the land of drought and heat,
> Where nothing grows for us to eat,
> For winds that blow with scorching heat,
> Nebraska Land is hard to beat.
> Oh, Nebraska Land! Sweet Nebraska Land!
> While on your burning soil I stand
> And look away across the plains
> And wonder why it never rains.
> Till Gabriel doth his trumpet sound
> They'll say the rain has gone around.

In 1895, things were better. The family moved again, this time to a tall house made of real lumber, not sod cut from the prairie. It was big enough so that, for the first time, they didn't have to keep a bed in the parlor.

As soon as Grace's mother finished work on her parlor so that she could be proud of the green blinds and cheesecloth curtains on the windows and a rag carpet padded with straw on the floor, a tremendous hail storm smashed the big windows and turned the curtains into limp rags.

Before bikinis ever shocked anybody, a new fashion arrived in Nebraska that caused dispproving comment. This was the bloomer, which came along with a craze for riding bicycles. Grace saved this description of the new style from a newspaper, the *Dawson County Pioneer:*

> The much talked about bloomer bicycle outfit for ladies is simply a pair of trousers very baggy at the knees, abnormally full about the pistol pocket and considerably loose where you would strike a match. The garment is cut decollet at the south end and the bottoms are tied around the knees to keep the mice out. You can't put it on over your head as you would a skirt, but you sit on the floor and pull it on just as you would put on your stockings, one foot in each compartment. You can easily tell which side to have in front by the button on the neck band.

Grace, sixteen that year, didn't even want bloomers, but she longed for a colored parasol. She bought it, twirled it gracefully, took it to a Fourth of July celebration, left it on the buggy seat—and somebody sat on it and broke the handle.

That year another girl baby arrived in the family. Grace and her sister Florrie, two years older, hadn't even known another baby was expected! Such things were not discussed, and their mother always wore a loose-fitting dress called a Mother Hubbard.

The family moved again, to a small house that was so filthy that every inch of the interior had to be scrubbed. Mr. McCance became very sick, probably with appendicitis, and almost died, because at that time doctors were afraid to operate. Abdominal operations were usually fatal. While Grace was caring for her father, one of her long-time dreams came true. She had always wanted to meet a cowboy. One came to the door to ask whether there was anything he could do to help. There wasn't.

Another dream almost came true. She had always wanted a birthday party, and when she turned eighteen she almost had one, but bad weather kept the invited guests away. She did have a cake with candles.

The ninth and last McCance baby was a boy. The house was full of big sisters who helped with his care and the other work, and Grace was free now to prepare for a career of teaching. She went to summer school, passed her examinations, and earned a teaching certificate. Her first school was one room in a farmhouse. She slept in it, sharing it with two little boys who were her pupils, taught in it and pieced quilts in it because her landlady wouldn't let her help with the housework—the teacher was much too exalted a person for that.

Grace didn't remain a teacher for very long. At twenty-one she married her cowboy, Bert Snyder, and began to run her own household. Her first baby was dead at birth; the second was a daughter, Nellie Irene, and the third was Miles William.

Nellie was ten and Miles was nine before they had a chance to go to school. Nebraska Land was settling up fast then and the world was changing. One big change resulted from a new homestead law, known as the Kinkaid Act, which became effective in 1904. Its chief backer was Moses P. Kinkaid, for twenty years a Congressman from Nebraska.

A homestead claim, at the time the McCances moved to Nebraska, was 160 acres, a quarter section. A hard-working man could make a living for his family with diversified farming on a place of that size. But in the sandhills of western Nebraska and in other arid country where cattle could be grazed but there wasn't enough rain to raise crops, a bigger acreage was needed. The Kinkaid Act permitted a homesteader to claim one section, a full square mile.

The homesteaders who poured into western Nebraska, where Grace's husband Bert raised cattle in the sandhills, were called Kinkaiders. Grace and Bert suddenly had a great many neighbors. Sod houses sprouted out of the sand like mushrooms after a rain.

The long-time settlers, like Bert Snyder, knew that even a full section of sandhill land was not enough for a Kinkaider to make a living. It wouldn't support enough cattle. Most of the newcomers had no cattle anyway. They came for free land, hoping to prove up and sell out at the end of five years.

Some cattlemen saw the Kinkaiders as a menace, because all these new claims decreased the amount of grazing that was available for the cattle that were already there. But in the Snyders' neighborhood, the cattlemen didn't fight the new-comers. Instead, they saw to it that the Kinkaiders didn't go hungry and, after they proved up, the cattlemen bought their land for needed pasture. Very few of the Kinkaiders became permanent settlers.

In 1912 the Snyders' second daughter was born. She was named Billie Lee because they had been planning on another boy. And something else joined the family that year. The Snyders bought their first automobile, a second-hand Ford for which they paid five hundred dollars. Roads were terrible then and for many years later. Automobiles weren't very good, and neither were tires. You had to be a fairly competent mechanic just to drive a car at that time, because you would probably have to make some repairs before you got to where you were going, only a few miles away.

The Snyders' first car had a black wooden body and a collapsible top, and the headlights needed gas to operate them. A team of horses—which could see at night, started without cranking, knew the way home, and didn't run out of fuel before they got there—really had a lot of advantages over an automobile!

Once Bert had to replace a cracked differential, and when he got through, the car ran backward.

In 1920, the twelve-year-old car broke down for the last time. They bought a new Ford, vastly improved. It had a metal body, a self-starter, and electric lights.

A couple of years later they had their first radio, built by son Miles from parts he ordered by mail. It was the wonder of the neighborhood. The radio ran on batteries (nobody yet dreamed of one that would work simply by being plugged into an electric outlet, let alone the portable transistor type), and it had no loudspeaker. It had two sets of headphones, and by dividing up the earpieces, four people at a time could listen to programs—if stormy weather didn't make the thing howl with static and if the batteries didn't go dead.

By the time Grace was fifty, she might have thought she had experienced about all the disasters that weather could bring. But on May 22, 1933, something new struck western Nebraska—a "black blizzard," a fierce dust storm of the kind from which Kansas, Colorado, and Oklahoma had already suffered.

At three o'clock in the afternoon, it was so dark that she told one of her girls to turn on the carbide lights while she ran out to see about her little turkeys. The dog was frightened—something was going to happen. The chickens had already gone to bed. Before Grace could persuade the turkey hen to take her babies under cover, a howling wind struck. Grace barely managed to get back inside the house. The kitchen floor seemed to be breathing, moving up and down in slow waves.

The wind went down within an hour, but they learned that a true tornado—never before known in the sandhills— had struck near them and had killed eight persons.

More dust storms followed, and pastures for cattle grew

smaller. The earth actually blew away, and where there was grass it was coated with dust. Cattle died of "dust-bowl pneumonia."

Thousands of ranchers and farmers went broke before rain came again. The Snyders were not hard hit, because Bert had enough pasture for his cattle. In 1940, however, the county they lived in had only 1,175 people in it. Thirty years before, the population had been 2,470.

During World War II, when tire and gasoline rationing made it impossble to travel very much, Grace pieced her finest quilts. One of them had 87,789 tiny pieces in it.

When Grace was eighty, she looked back on her life and wrote a book, *No Time on My Hands,* published in 1963.

"I couldn't have asked for a more wonderful eighty years to live in," she said.

Postscript

While doing the research for this book, the author came across such fascinating details on the domestic arrangements of the times that they are included here for the benefit of readers interested in the lot of the harried housekeeper.

Most families in the nineteenth century lived on farms, miles from a doctor, even if they didn't live out west on the frontier. When sickness struck, they depended on home remedies. Many of them prudently kept a "doctor book" which, along with the Bible, might constitute the entire household library. (There might also be a couple of McGuffey's readers, used by one child after another in country school.)

One such doctor book was *Dr. Chase's Family Physician, Farrier, Bee-keeper, and Second Receipt Book.* Receipt is an old word for recipe.

Dr. Chase, who was a printer, not a doctor of medicine, earnestly tried to tell his readers how to solve all their home and farm problems. His book tells how to concoct medicines;

how to make axle grease, ink, soap, yeast, and dozens of other things; how to raise bees; and how to treat sick horses—the last-named item explains the "Farrier" part of the title.

Dr. Chase thought bathing was a fine thing; he recommended it in eleven pages of fine print. He included pictures of bathtubs of various kinds for the instruction of readers whose only personal experience involved folding awkwardly into a too-small washtub on Saturday night.

The worthy Dr. Chase was ahead of his time on the topic of bathing, and he was also very progressive in the cooking recipes he included. (He must have got them from progressive housewives.) Measurements of ingredients were vague in most recipes then—a pinch of this, "sufficient" of something else, "a small amount" of the next thing. Most recipe compilers never dreamed of telling how to combine the ingredients. Cream the butter and sugar together, beat the eggs and add them, alternate the milk and flour—those tricks you were just supposed to *know*.

It is only since the invention of electric mixers that the lady in the kitchen can dump all the measured ingredients for a cake into a bowl and let machinery do a job that used to require both planning and a strong right arm.

You can thank Fannie Farmer, who was born in 1857, for standardizing measurements. She became director of the Boston Cooking School. Now, a cup is a measuring cup, and a teaspoon is a measuring teaspoon. Nobody needs to guess how much a teacup or a dessert spoon holds or estimate "a lump of butter the size of an egg." A kitchen no longer needs a scale for weighing pounds of sugar or flour.

Some of Dr. Chase's solutions seem worse than the problems. His "receipt" for getting rid of ants involved wetting a sponge, putting fine sugar on it to attract the little crawlers, and then dropping the sponge in boiling water twice a day.

If the housewife lived long enough, she might outlast all the
ants.

If you have a yearning to make your own yeast, here's all
you have to do. This recipe, quoted by Dr. Chase from *Oliver
Optic's Magazine,* was called "Yeast—in Rhyme—Very Fine"
—but "very fine" does not apply to the quality of the verse.

A handful of fragrant hops deposit in a kettle;
Then add a pint of Adams' Ale° and boil them till they
    settle;
Then if you wish to brew good Yeast, lively and sweet, you'd
    oughter
Take four potatoes, medium sized, and wash them well with
    water;
Divest them of their jackets next—in common parlance,
    skin 'em—
And faithfully dig out the eyes—there's dirt embedded in
    'em—
Then make assurance doubly sure and banish all pollution,
By subsequently giving them another grand ablution;
Then boil them, half an hour, perhaps; of course, your
    judgment using,
Or steam them, if you like it best; the method's of your
    choosing.
But whether boiled or cooked by steam the process should be
    rapid;
Potatoes moderately cooked are heavy, soggy, vapid.
Then mash them thoroughly, each lump with vigor pulveriz-
    ing,
And put them in a vessel which leaves ample room for
    rising;
A cup half filled with sugar add; 'twill sweeten it enough.
It needs the same amount of salt; you'll find it *quantum suff*
    [sufficient quantity];

• Water

The hop infusion strain in next, a pint, you mind, by meas-
ure;
Then with two quarts of water warm, dilute it at your
pleasure,
And to gently keeping it moving, from circumference to
center,
Never fail to bid your *silver* spoon its hidden depth to enter;
Then add two brimming cups of Yeast, and quickly take
occasion
The fragrant mixture to subject to brisk manipulation.
And, when the entire ingredients are mingled well together,
Then give the opportunity to rise, according to the weather—
In Winter set it near the stove, and oft renew the fire;
In Summer place it farther off; the temperature is higher—
Then patiently the issue wait, while Time his flight is wing-
ing,
Its status scanning now and then, and when you hear it
singing,
And see upon its surface—now here, now there—a bubble,
You'll feel a thousand-fold repaid for all your time and trou-
ble.
Give to the winds all idle fears; all doubts, all scruples
banish;
And when the bubbles thicken fast, and crowd, and break,
and vanish,
The Yeast is prime, your toil is o'er, success has crowned
persistence,
And loaves of tender, light sweet bread are looming in the
distance.

Ah, but your toil *isn't* o'er. You just have the yeast. Now
you make the bread. For seven small loaves, take about two-
thirds of a common milk pan of sour milk (of course you
keep a cow, so you *have* sour milk), scald it, and pour off the
whey. Save it. When this whey is cooled to "milk warm," sift

the flour and stir it in—the recipe doesn't hint at how much flour—with a cup of the hop yeast and let it rise overnight. In the morning, knead in "the proper amount" of sifted flour, let it rise again, knead it, make it into loaves, let them rise properly, and then bake.

The recipe doesn't say how long to bake or how hot the oven should be. These things you just know, because your mother taught you. She also taught you how to regulate the oven heat, more or less, by judicious use of damper and draft on the stove, supposing you were prosperous enough to own a stove.

That yeast you just made required hops and brewers yeast. Suppose you couldn't get them? You could still make yeast. Boil half a pound of flour, two ounces of brown sugar, a gallon of water, and a teaspoon of salt.

Dr. Chase gave "receipts" for homemade dyes. Most of them call for ingredients that you'd have a hard time getting now. One way to dye goods yellow was this: Boil your goods for an hour in alum (four ounces for each pound of fabric) and cream of tartar (one ounce for each pound), with enough water to cover. Empty the kettle, fill with clean water, put in a pound of fustic for each pound of fabric, boil for another hour, then rinse. Fustic came from tropical jungle trees, but you could make do with osage orange, common in some parts of the United States.

After all that effort, you deserve to be the belle of the ball in that yellow dress.

If you had kept house on the frontier, or on a farm even in the early years of the present century, after the frontier was gone, you would have made your own soap instead of choosing among dozens of packages on the shelves in a supermarket.

For hard soap, first make up a batch of caustic lye by mix-

ing a pound of caustic soda and a pound of stone lime in half
a gallon of water. Boil this and pour off the clear lye to use.
(This recipe gives only the proportions. You would use
greater quantities.)

Next put a lot of the caustic lye into three gallons of
water with six pounds of clean lard or tallow saved from the
last time your men folks butchered. Boil this until it's thick,
pour into a wooden box, and cut it up into neat chunks after
it gets cold and hard. For soap chips, get out a knife and
patiently shave a chunk of your product.

If you don't want to waste clean lard, which you made with
much toil from hog fat, or if you don't have any tallow (the
fat of sheep or cattle), you can use "any of the coarser fats,"
an old recipe says, without specifying what they are, plus a
pound or two of rosin for each pound of fat. This makes
yellow soap that doesn't wear out so fast on the washboard.

Lard was the only shortening and cooking fat there was. No
vegetable fats were made. In a pinch, you could make lard
from a bear's fat, but let's say you had raised some hogs for
their meat. You "tried out" the fat in a great iron kettle over
a fire out of doors to avoid saturating the house with the odor.

Most women dreaded slaughtering time. They shuddered
at the sound of the pigs' screams as their throats were cut,
and they hated the hot, smelly work of trying out lard.

Even in the early years of the present century, some housewives who didn't have to worry about the problems of frontier living made their own starch. Starch comes in a pres-
surized can, now, and when you iron you simply spray it on
anything that needs stiffening. But *Household Discoveries
and Mrs. Curtis's Cook Book*, published in 1908, gives in-
structions for grating raw potatoes into water, squeezing
the mass in cheese cloth, and letting the thicker part settle.

The clear liquid on top was handy for cleaning delicate

fabrics; what settled to the bottom was starch; and the potato
fibers that were strained out were good for washing carriage
robes and horse blankets. *Household Discoveries* also recognized store-bought starch—and enough variations in ironing
to explain why housekeeping was a full-time job in 1908.

"The electric flatiron," we are told, "is an ideal utensil
in homes that are supplied with electricity"—and that's all
we learn about this new-fangled contraption. Solid flatirons,
which had to be held with a pad around the handle, were
still standard equipment.

That wasn't all you needed if you took proper pride in the
appearance of your family's clothes. You needed a polishing
iron to make the bosoms, collars, and cuffs of men's shirts
really shine. For fine tucks and puffy sleeves, you should have
a puff iron. You could borrow your little girl's toy iron for
tucks and fluting.

Not so long ago, frugality, like cleanliness, was considered
close to godliness. Every scrap of everything was utilized—or
put away to save until some use for it developed. Scraps of
fabric too tiny to be used for anything else were sewed together for quilt tops or cut into strips, sewed together, and
braided into rugs.

Small quantities of left-over food were put away to be
served again to the family or were welcomed by dogs and cats,
which hadn't learned to expect patented pet food in cans.

When a woman made a garment, she expected to mend it
and patch it and then make it over, either for herself or for
one of the children.

Household Discoveries recommends making two house
dresses of the same material. When they show wear, the book
advises, rip them apart and make them over into one dress,
and you may have enough left over for a couple of aprons.
Any woman who could afford two new dresses at once would

prbably think twice before deciding to have even the prettiest print around for that many years of wear.

The Household Discoveries part of this book has 675 pages. It tells everything about everything around the house —how to measure and hem your own sheets, how to make dish cloths of raveled rope. If you insist on using kerosene to get the kitchen fire going in a hurry, at least have the wits not to blow up the stove by pouring the fluid right from the can onto the hot coals.

No doubt the book was a fine wedding present. But many a promised bride, leafing through all those pages that told her how to be a good housekeeper, must have wondered if it wouldn't be less exhausting to stay single and keep on teaching school.

Bibliography

Adair, Bethenia Owens. *Dr. Owens-Adair: Some of Her Life Experiences.* Portland, Oregon: Mann & Beach, 1906.

Alderson, Nannie T., and Helena Huntington Smith. *A Bride Goes West.* New York: Farrar & Rinehart, 1942.

Andrist, Ralph K. *The Long Death.* New York: The Macmillan Company, 1964.

Bagley, Clarence. *Early Catholic Missions in Old Oregon.* Two volumes. Seattle: Lowman & Hanford Co., 1932.

Barsness, Larry. *Gold Camp.* New York: Hastings House, 1962.

Bird, Isabella L. *A Lady's Life in the Rocky Mountains.* Norman: University of Oklahoma Press, 1960.

Conant, Roger. *Mercer's Belles,* edited by Lenna A. Deutsch. Seattle: University of Washington Press, 1960.

Custer, Elizabeth B. *Boots and Saddles or, Life in Dakota with General Custer.* Norman: University of Oklahoma Press, 1961.

Darling, Lucia. Untitled manuscript journal of the Sanders-Edgerton journey from Tallmadge, Ohio, to Bannack, Idaho Territory, 1863. Private collection of William Bertsche, Great Falls, Montana.

DeShields, James T. *Cynthia Ann Parker.* St. Louis, 1886. Privately published.

Dimsdale, Prof. Thos J. *The Vigilantes of Montana.* Fourth edition. Helena, Montana: State Publishing Company. No date. Edited by A. J. Noyes.

Drury, Clifford Merrill. *Elkanah and Mary Walker, Pioneers*

Among the Spokanes. Caldwell, Idaho: The Caxton Printers, 1940.

Engle, Flora A. P. "The Story of the Mercer Expedition." *The Washington Historical Quarterly,* Vol. VI, No. 4, October 1915.

Foster-Harris. *The Look of the Old West.* New York: The Viking Press, 1955.

Grinnell, George Bird. *The Fighting Cheyennes.* London: Chapman and Hall, 1896.

Hutchens, John K. *One Man's Montana.* Philadelphia and New York: J. B. Lippincott Company, 1964.

In Harvest Fields by Sunset Shores: The Work of the Sisters of Notre Dame on the Pacific Coast. By a member of the congregation. No author's name. San Francisco: Gilmartin, 1926.

Jackson, Grace. *Cynthia Ann Parker.* San Antonio: The Naylor Company, 1959.

Johnson, Virginia W. *The Unregimented General.* Boston: Houghton Mifflin Co., 1962.

Kelly, Fanny. *Narrative of My Captivity Among the Sioux Indians.* Chicago: Donnelley, Gassette & Lloyd, 1880.

Langford, N. P. *Vigilante Days and Ways.* Missoula: Montana State University Press, 1957.

Lass, William E. *A History of Steamboating on the Upper Missouri River.* Lincoln: University of Nebraska Press, 1962.

McCrosson, Sister Mary of the Blessed Sacrament. *The Bell and the River.* Palo Alto: Pacific Books, 1957.

McKee, Ruth Karr. *Mary Richardson Walker: Her Book.* Caldwell, Idaho: The Caxton Printers, Ltd., 1945.

Meredith, Grace E. *Girl Captives of the Cheyennes.* Los Angeles: Gem Publishing Co., 1927.

Miles, Nelson A. *Personal Recollections.* Chicago: Werner & Co., 1896.

Miller, David Humphreys. "Sitting Bull's White Squaw." *Montana, The Magazine of Western History,* Vol. 14, No. 2, Spring, 1964.

Mooney, James. *The Ghost-Dance Religion.* Extract from the Fourteenth Annual Report of the Bureau of Ethnology. Washington: Government Printing Office, 1896.

Palladino, L. B. *Indian and White in the Northwest.* Second Edition. Lancaster, Pennsylvania: Wickersham Publishing Co., 1922.

Parker, James W. *Narrative of the Perilous Adventures, Miraculous Escapes and Sufferings of Rev. James W. Parker, During a Frontier Residence in Texas, of Fifteen Years . . . to which is appended a Narrative of the Capture and Subsequent Sufferings of Mrs. Rachel Plummer, his daughter.* Palestine, Texas: 1926 (reprint of 1844 original).

Peckham, Howard H. *Captured by Indians.* New Brunswick: Rutgers University Press, 1954.

Sanders, Harriet Peck Fenn, Manuscript journals in the private collection of William Bertsche, Great Falls, Montana.

———, James U., Manuscript journals in the private collection of William Bertsche, Great Falls, Montana.

Schmitt, Martin F., and Dee Brown. *Fighting Indians of the West.* New York: Charles Scribner's Sons, 1948.

Stewart, Edgar I. *Custer's Luck.* Norman: University of Oklahoma Press, 1955.

Tate, Mildred Thurow, and Oris Glisson. *Family Clothing.* New York and London: John Wiley & Sons, Inc., 1961.

Vestal, Stanley. *New Sources of Indian History.* Norman: University of Oklahoma Press, 1934.

———. *Sitting Bull, Champion of the Sioux.* Norman: University of Oklahoma Press, 1956.

Webb, Todd. *The Gold Rush Trail and the Road to Oregon.* Garden City: Doubleday & Co., 1963.

Wheeler, Col. Homer W. *Buffalo Days.* Indianapolis: The Bobbs-Merrill Company, 1923.

Snyder, Grace. *No Time on My Hands.* As told to Nellie Snyder Yost. Caldwell, Idaho: The Caxton Printers, Ltd., 1963.

Index

Indian burial custom, 119
Indian dresses, 27
Indians, government treatment of, 50,
   51, 110, 111, 123-126
Indian transportation methods, 14
Ironing, 173
Ives, George, trial of, 67

Kelly, Fanny, 8-21
Kelly, Josiah, 9-21
Kinkaid Aid, 162
Kinkaiders, 162 ff.

Laundry problems, 62, 63, 140, 156 ff.
Little Bighorn, Battle of, 126, 127

Mail delivery, 68
Mary, niece of Fanny Kelly, 9-20
McLaughlin, Major James, 131 ff.
Mercer, Asa, 53-57
"Mercer's Belles," 53-57
Medical education, 93, 94
Miles City, Montana Territory, 139 ff.
Miles, General Nelson A., 30 ff.
Montana Post, 68-71
Montgomery Ward, 148

Nebraska, farming in, 151-165
Nevada City, Montana Territory, 66
Nugent, "Mountain Jim," 107-114
Nuns, 47-52

Ottawa, Sioux chief, 12-17
Owens-Adair, Dr. Bethenia, 85-99

Parker, Cynthia Ann, 1-5
Parker, James, 1, 2, 3
Patterns for sewing, 141
Pease River, Battle of, 4
Peta Nocona, Comanche chief, 4
Plummer, Electa Bryan, 76-79
Plummer, James, 2, 3
Plummer, Rachel, 2
Plummer, Sheriff Henry, 66, 76-79
Political activity of women, 97, 98
Politics in America, 103
Prairie fire, 154

Preloch, Indian name of Cynthia Ann
   Parker, 4
Protestant missionaries, 36-46

Quanah, son of Cynthia Ann Parker,
   5 ff.

Radio, 164
Rattlesnakes, 143
Riding costume, 119, 142
Road ranches, 139
Robbers' Roost, 78, 79
Ross, Captain Sul, 4

Sailing ship travel, 54-55
St. Ignatius Mission, 48-52
Sanders, Harriet, 58-75
Sanders, James, 59 ff.
Sanders, Wilbur Fisk, 58-75
Sanders, Willie (Wilbur), 59 ff.
Savoie, Jules, 81
Scalp dance, 14
Scandals in President Grant's admin-
   istration, 124-125
Schools, 48-52, 87, 91, 153 ff., 162
Sears, Roebuck, 149
Sewing machines, 142
Shawls, 63
Sidesaddle, 98
Sioux Indians, starvation among, 130
Sister Mary of the Infant Jesus, 48 ff.
Sisters of Providence, 47-52
Sitting Bull, 129-136
Slade, Joseph Albert, 79-83
Slade, Maria Virginia, 79-84
Snyder, Bert, 162 ff.
Snyder, Grace McCance, 150-165
Soap making, 171, 172
Sod house, 150 ff.
Stagecoach travel, 72, 73
Starch making, 172
Steamship travel, 72-74
Sully, General Alfred, 14
Sun Dance, 134
Sunday School, 156

Thanksgiving celebration, 113
Thread making, 87